TACKLING THE GAME

TACKLING THE GAME

PAUL PARKER

MY LIFE IN FOOTBALL

pitch

First published by Pitch Publishing, 2025
1

Pitch Publishing
9 Donnington Park,
85 Birdham Road,
Chichester, West Sussex,
PO20 7AJ

www.pitchpublishing.co.uk
info@pitchpublishing.co.uk

A CIP catalogue record is available for this book from the British Library.

ISBN 978 1 83680 188 7

Typesetting and origination by Pitch Publishing

MIX
Paper | Supporting responsible forestry
FSC® C013604

Printed and bound in the UK on FSC® certified paper in line with our continuing commitment to ethical business practices, sustainability and the environment.

Printed and bound by CPI Group (UK) Ltd, Croydon, CR0 4YY

Contents

Introduction 7

1. Dealing with Racism. 19

2. Learning the Hard Way 30

3. Ups and Downs at Fulham. 45

4. The Top Tier with QPR 54

5. The World Cup in Italy 69

6. Moving North 87

7. All Change for England 105

8. Early Disappointment at United 113

9. Changes, and a Certain Frenchman 141

10. Training Days 152

11. The First Title 169

12. The Boss is Always Right 190

13. A United Bond 207

14. Our Own Piece of History 219

15. Breaking Down 238

16. The Hard Goodbye 253

17. Falling Out of and Back in Love with the Game 264

18. Essex, via Singapore, via Darwin 277

Introduction

IT'S SAID that a person is the product of the experiences of their life. That's probably true, but when I was thinking of that as a way to start this book, I'd say I was probably more influenced by the people I've met along the way. It would be fair to say the majority of those experiences came in my younger days but I know that throughout my life, even up to this present day, I continue to meet people who influence and add something to my life.

The obvious place to start is my family. I'm writing this book with the awareness that I've already written one before, so I don't wish to repeat myself. People write a book and start from the beginning, so their family life usually forms a part of that. I know I'm very much influenced by my parents and my siblings, even if we don't live in each other's pockets. We're all like that; there's four kids and all of us are individuals in what we do. We're not constantly ringing each other. That would maybe stem from the fact that we came out of East London. It was a fight for survival, I'd say … maybe that's a bit deep, but we had our own little battles to fight because of where we'd come from.

We were a black family moving to a predominantly white area, a council house estate. Our parents had come over in the Windrush generation and my siblings and I were second generation. Let's just say people had their own ideas of acceptance. My sister and brothers and I were all different ages, so we went to different schools. It was very, very difficult. My sister went to a school with more black and Indian people in it. I went to a school where it was tough if you weren't white. I'm making the point of comparison not to say one had it worse than the other, only to say our experiences were different, if similar. We all suffered racist abuse. Those personal battles, those unique individual circumstances provided the impetus for all of us to dig deep and look after ourselves first more than anything, really. In that, we were alike. We got on with it. We didn't come home and sulk. We just got on with it. I couldn't say we accepted it, because that's not the right word, but we knew we had nowhere to go.

Today there are different organisations and even government bodies to help with racism, and people feel that they can go to them. I'd say that's a good thing, if people feel helped by them, but I do always ask the question of how much someone in an organisation really cares, because, at the end of the day, they're getting paid quite well for it. That wasn't the climate we were raised in. I'd like to think my generation were all the stronger for what we went through and my opinion is that it made us more resilient.

While I'd say we had to deal with many things in our own way, I know that I have characteristics shared by my family. Even down to our sense of home. My parents moved to England. I've lived away from them since the age of 15. I never went backwards. Neither did they. I was chasing a dream and so were they, though I've got to say it would have been extremely difficult for them leaving big families.

My dad was one of nine kids. He's been back home once. My mum hasn't been back at all – she just didn't want to. She was the proudest woman in the world to get her British passport. They're both very proud of their roots but Mum developed a great protection of the Queen; she built a strong respect for a country that invited my mum and dad here. That was never anything said to us explicitly, it was just obvious in the way that she conducted herself. There was class and dignity and respect for the place she now called home.

I've lived abroad and experienced what it could be like if you didn't respect the local culture or behaviour. It makes communication tremendously difficult and can turn people against you or make them ignore you. It wasn't so much in the way it was impressed on me, more something I naturally adopted from the way my mum conducted herself. Mum never acted as though she was owed anything, and neither did Dad; so as they've got older, and my respect for them has probably grown even more, I've wanted to make sure they have the best quality of life possible. They made a sacrifice for us to have a better life; a sacrifice in leaving all they knew, when they knew they might not be able to return even if they wanted to, and a sacrifice in living in times of personal struggle, of placing themselves in an environment that was frequently abusive and volatile in order to eventually create and provide a better life.

That being said, it would be a brave person who'd take my mum on, all 4ft 11in of her. Be careful what you say around her. She says what she thinks, to the extent that she was worried that she might lose the job she had at Lyon's tea shops, and therefore risk being sent back. Thankfully it didn't come to that and it didn't change my mum. If we were going to Romford, the only black family on the bus, and we got a dirty look, she'd let them have it. It didn't matter how much smaller she was. She wouldn't let anyone talk down to her, or us. She didn't stand for anything that might make us feel disrespected. As someone who didn't let their size limit them in their life and career, I can safely say that was an attitude I got from her, and I'm proud to say that.

There are traits I share with my sister and brothers, mostly the way we'd fight against adversity. My sister, as the eldest of us, was quite a powerhouse. My brothers are fighters. I loved a challenge. I'd walk three miles to training in Dagenham and back, and save the bus fare money for sweets, even though around that time there were plenty of people from the National Front or British Movement around. You had to be constantly aware, looking out for skinheads. I trained with Arsenal for a while and would leave at around ten o'clock when the pubs were emptying. There was a skinhead pub near Highbury; I'd have to hide inside the tube station and then run to get the bus as soon as I saw it coming. Then, depending on if I'd already spent my bus fare, I might try to hide from the conductor and jump off before being caught. I walked everywhere. When most people did their paper round on their bikes, well, I didn't have one, so I got my £2.50 a week doing that or bob-a-job around people's houses doing whatever odd jobs they wanted done.

We were latch-key kids. Mum ran everything in the house. The one thing you'd never want to do is upset her, because you'd be terrified of Dad when he came home from work. My dad, well I could say my love of football probably came from him. And apart from my family, most of the influential people in my life were involved in my football career. There are so many people I could name, people who took me almost into their families. There was a bloke called Tommy Reader, whose son Wayne played for West Ham and won the Youth Cup with them in 1981. I was playing for Romford Juniors and we played against Wayne, and somehow I connected with the dad by playing against the team that his son played for. Then there was my good friend Steve Martin (still a good friend to this day). His dad took me in when I was about 11. There was Tommy South, who owned Purfleet Football Club, which became Thurrock Football Club. I still know Tommy – when I played in the World Cup in Italy in 1990 he came out and followed me around. I remember seeing him in Sardinia. There are a lot of people I've maintained contact with from my very early days in football, even if we don't speak all the time. When we do, it's like we spoke yesterday, and those are probably the people who understand me best.

While there are people I remember and keep in touch with, there are obviously certain people whose influence on my life is more obvious, something I can look at and notice where my life changed. Johnny Martin brought me to a team who played in Dagenham, at a higher level of football than I was used to. From playing against local Essex teams, I was playing against London sides on a more competitive and highly intense level. The players you're playing against are all district level, county level players, most of them.

Ray Harford was the man who gave me the opportunity to become a professional at Fulham. I don't know why he took me on board, but there was something about our relationship where Ray seemed to love to hate me. Hate's a little strong. Maybe dislike is better. He always said he hated wasted talent and it was a saying that stayed with me. Talent is great, he'd say. He'd talk about the attribute he loved but could never be relied upon, because all you've got to do is trip over, and then you've lost it – pace. His preaching to me was that you can't be reliant on things. You have to make things happen for yourself.

When I moved to Queens Park Rangers, I was a Third Division player moving to the top flight. Jim Smith showed faith in me at a time when the First Division was packed with quality English players. Even to make the national squad was a massive achievement. As a schoolboy, I couldn't get anywhere near international football. I was deemed too small. It was very, very, very competitive. So Jim Smith took a chance and saw something in me. It was certainly something only he saw, because he made a decision that shocked everyone, to play me in the middle of defence. He did that off his own back. I don't know whether or not he was looking for something different, but I think, during pre-season, he decided that he was going to play me in the middle. I did that in my first game, against West Ham at Upton Park. Not once during my time at Queens Park Rangers did I play as a full-back or a wing-back. I was always in the middle. His decision redirected my career and enhanced my reputation. Yes, you have to make things happen for yourself. If you do that to the best of your ability then you can be prepared for luck, or fate, to hopefully help you out. I'm not saying I was lucky to get where I got to. I made the most of what I had but I benefitted from the foresight and intervention of others, which moved my life and career to a different stage. Jim certainly did that.

The most obvious name here is Alex Ferguson, and his decision to sign me for Manchester United. Do I need to explain why? Everyone wanted to do that. Everyone wanted to play for Manchester United. It was the name. It was just something about it. As a schoolboy in the 1970s, you might say the club was being talked about for the wrong reasons. But still, they had the swagger about them by their name. My mum and dad knew the name. My dad knew who George Best, Bobby Charlton, Denis Law were. That was his side. He loved cricket – Viv Richards, Clive Lloyd and Garry Sobers from his love of West Indian cricket. But he loved United. I signed for them and my life changed.

It's about your hard work, the intervention of others. And timing. I didn't find out until later in my career that United had wanted to sign me when I was at Fulham. Jimmy Murphy had apparently recommended me to Ron Atkinson in 1985. I didn't know about that – I knew about an offer from Liverpool. But the Fulham chairman Ernie Clay liked me, and he didn't want to let me go. Ernie was a distinctive man. Broad Yorkshire accent. In West London he stood out. He didn't want to sell me – he asked for something like an extra £50,000 when it seemed like Liverpool thought they'd already agreed a fee. They said no, they wouldn't go overboard for potential.

So I might have joined United earlier if they'd have put in a bid. I'm asked about my regrets in football and I've said that I regret not being at United maybe a year earlier, so I could have been involved in that European Cup Winners' Cup team. The whole buzz when I arrived was about the Cup Winners' Cup; there were all these different little events going on, and almost as soon as I arrived I was sitting in the room with all my new team-mates who were getting suited and booted to go to this event to mark the win, and I was waving goodbye to them. 'I'll see you at training tomorrow,' I said, desperate to have been a part of it. Desperate, from what I'd seen, to have been a part of everything in Rotterdam. It was a big thing for the club, it was definitely massive for the boss, something to build on, but then I realised what that was like in my following seasons, seeing new players arrive, and there were always things going on because of United being what they are. You'd win something, and it doesn't matter how small it seems to be from the outside, they'd treat winning everything with respect.

I was still learning then. But, I have to say, I'm glad that I joined United when I did. I won my first-ever medal at professional level in my first season. I should have had two winners' medals that season, but for me it was a massive step forward. It changed my life in a way that I'm not sure I can fully articulate – you move from football club to football club, and this is no slight or disrespect meant to any other, but you realise after you join United, and especially after you leave, that your life *becomes* Manchester United. Your life is football but your association with United is even bigger, due to the fact that it's the biggest club in the world.

My dream of being a footballer started from when I was six or seven, from just playing in the back garden. My friend Ian, who lived across the road, introduced me to the cubs, so I joined the cubs to play football on Saturday mornings. Incidentally, in the early part of 2024, the grandson of the old manager was trying to track me down. He'd passed away and they were going through all his stuff. He'd kept a count of every single game, of every player, and they found stuff on me, because back then I was their record goalscorer. That was my introduction, but if you're going to play any proper football, it comes on Sunday mornings when you're young. I ended up joining a team called Pegasus, which was a local Upminster/Hornchurch team, and they wore yellow and green. I played as a winger for them before getting headhunted, if that's the right word to use in football, by Romford Juniors. At the age of 11 is when it starts to get a bit nasty. You go on to full-size pitches, and a lot of kids weren't physically or mentally ready for it. The football changes, the adults change, their personalities change.

Nowadays, every parent wants their kid to be a footballer because of the money, and every kid wants the fame. We were brought up watching individual players and heroes. Frank Worthington and Stan Bowles were flamboyant forwards with lots of skill. You didn't get to see a lot of football on television, so the memories of watching them were mostly from cup finals. Liverpool were on television often because they were winning so much, so I remember loving the way Kenny Dalglish played. You'd go straight into the garden and try to imitate him. The glamour game always seemed to be Spurs vs United. I have such a vivid memory of watching them play on *The Big Match*, with Brian Moore commentating. Spurs had this swagger about them, always doing well in the FA Cup, which was the big televised game. There were Garth Crooks and Steve Archibald in their team. Glenn Hoddle, when he was a young player. Steve Perryman, too.

I might have signed for Spurs, but ended up going to United. I was fortunate enough to win enough silverware at Old Trafford that meant I was more successful than the heroes of my childhood, and that's a peculiar feeling to look back on. When I joined United, they'd won in Europe, but they hadn't won the league for almost a quarter of a century. There was no guarantee of what would happen. The reason why I wanted to go to Manchester United was because you have to go to the best. If you fail, you can never be questioned, because you've gone there and you've tried; you can always go back, knowing that you gave everything to go forward, and you'll be respected for that.

I could have turned around and said I didn't want to leave QPR. It's easy to sit there and be comfortable. You have to be brave to take on what goes with it, because as much as many players achieved at Manchester United, there are a lot of players that didn't achieve as well, and it wasn't because they weren't good enough, it was the pressure. What you had to achieve at a club like Manchester United was winning, and doing it to a certain standard. Your standards as a person and footballer. The best feeling ever is to know that you've stepped up and you're approached by a coach or a manager to congratulate you. You don't want a manager to sense that you're even close to the comfort zone. There was one manager who knew how to deal with that attitude ruthlessly. You know who I mean. You have to be brave. You have to be committed. For yourself, and to justify the faith of the people who influenced the journey to help you get to where you are. This is true of my career but is applicable to anyone on their own journey.

To get there, for me, the only way I could be was to be all-in. There was nothing else for me. I was totally single-minded about it. It's said that you stand a far greater chance of succeeding in a dream if it's the only thing you visualise. Becoming a professional footballer was the fulfilment of a dream. I quickly learned to realise that accomplishing a dream like that has a danger – you can fall into the comfort zone. That's human nature. Then come the attacks. The criticisms. The setbacks. Do you have the personality and the ability to rise to that challenge? You can listen to the criticism and sulk about it; you can let it affect you. You have to realise at that point that you're giving the critic what they want. Can you stand up to it – the internal demon, the external demon – and excel before the critic, circumstance or complacency takes a toll … or before somebody else makes the decision for you?

1
Dealing with Racism

THERE WAS a lad who had the old Robinson Jam logo on his lapel and his blazer. He was far from the only one who was openly showing his ignorance. And I think I was far from the only black kid who'd have to run all the way home, almost three miles, across the old airfield at Hornchurch Aerodrome, jumping through mud, getting our trousers ripped after catching them on some rocks or a fence.

At school I'd get called names. All of the names. Did it bother me? Of course it did. But ten minutes later I'd shrug it off and forget it, because I had my mates around me. They were all white. Did I want them to stand up, to say something, to stop it? No. First, I didn't want anyone to fight my battles for me. I didn't want them to get involved. I'd see them all before school and we'd all go together. One of my mates gave me his bike – a very expensive bike – which he'd got from his dad, who was a single parent and had worked hard to give it to him. My mate knew he'd get a rollicking off his dad but gave me the bike to make sure I got home alright. I had to believe in that saying about sticks and stones. Words hurt me but didn't affect me. Actions might have, if they'd have grabbed hold of me, but that never happened, thankfully. I never found out how far someone was willing to go.

I quickly accepted it. I didn't have a choice. I felt that, if I had, I'd have been questioned as a person. I didn't go to my mum and dad about it. Could I have done? Should I have done? Yeah, maybe. But they were working every hour they could to put food on the table. They couldn't afford the time to come to school and complain about something that was much bigger than them. Bigger than the schools and the teachers. They were facing the same thing at their own work. My sister and brothers were too.

In the late 1970s, the BBC aired a programme called *Roots*, which was about slavery in the United States. I remember that, while it aired, and afterwards, there was a really toxic racist atmosphere at school, almost like the programme had weaponised or provoked them. I guarantee that every black kid of my age would have suffered with abuse because of that programme. The lead character was called Kunta Kinte and that was what I was called. In the show he has his foot cut off to stop him escaping. My sister got called Kizzy because that was the name of one of the other characters.

We went to school every day. I don't think I ever missed a day. I didn't know it at the time, this was not the mindset I had at the time, but it's obvious looking back that none of those kids really understood what they were saying or doing. They were products of their environment, repeating what they'd heard elsewhere, being kids, trying to get a reaction. And they did get a reaction from me, but just not a direct one. It gave me adversity and it provided me with something to prove myself against.

It was ignorance. Children aren't born racist; they're taught that sort of behaviour by parents, grandparents. I still remember the first time I went round to my ex-wife's house. I was about 17 or 18. We were having spaghetti bolognese. I didn't know how to eat it. Her granddad was there, and I went and sat in the front room with him after eating. He started talking, about the war, and he brought out the word wogs. I was sitting there open-mouthed when my girlfriend's dad came in and had to explain that he'd meant it referring to Italians. I just kind of froze, and it wasn't said again. Reflecting on that now, is it fair that I had to shoulder the burden of understanding? Maybe not. Yes, it was a bizarre situation, having it explained that he's not being racist, he's being xenophobic, and you're not the target, so that's meant to be okay. The modern retaliation is to hold somebody accountable and that means destroying their livelihood on the back of it. Did the grandfather mean any malice, or did he say the wrong word at the wrong time? Did he just need to be educated?

Racism is still a problem. But I believe it's a smaller problem as the world has become smaller, and I'm speaking over the course of generations, with interracial marriages and immigration. I speak from experience as someone who lived in Singapore for a few years. My kids went to school there. One day after school, one of my boys ran up to me and said he was going to stay with one of his friends, an Indian boy, and pointed him out – he pointed him out by his trainers. I do believe that with each passing generation, racism is becoming a smaller issue in society.

However, it does remain an issue, and a high-profile one at that. Football is one of the most high-profile platforms that has a vehicle for fighting racism, and multiple vehicles for it to be seen. Maybe I was lucky, because I was so obsessed with sports, and I wasn't bad at it. That changed things for me, it changed the way I was seen. It helped me build relationships. Some might say it shouldn't be that way. Maybe so, but that was my life. Sport, for me, was a way to relate. Relating made communicating easier. In a lot of sports, you have to work with people. All the sports I was involved in, I was always with other people. So I had to converse. All of a sudden, people find that except for the bit that they can see on the outside, I'm no different on the inside.

I look back today on the last 40 or 50 years and my opinion is that attitudes towards racism have improved, at least on a living, everyday level, so much in that time. Black footballers started to feature more prominently in top-flight teams in the late 70s and I was no different to most in that I looked upon players like Laurie Cunningham, Brendon Batson and Cyrille Regis as gods. Those three, and Clyde Best, who played for West Ham, really got my dad's interest into football from cricket. They definitely paved the way, but I was so single-minded that already by then I was determined that it would be me and me alone who'd determine whether or not I'd be a professional. I do confess that Laurie Cunningham was a little bit different because we'd see him on the streets of Hornchurch because he was seeing a girl around town – I think he actually married her. But here was a player who captured headlines, who played brilliantly. He was such a superb athlete. And he went on to play for Real Madrid and Manchester United. He had the character to go to Spain and go through everything there. He just looked to Real Madrid, and he just went, I've got to go. He challenged himself every single time and it was a challenge again for him on and off the park. I probably was inspired by that, because that's how I looked at it, to be perfectly honest.

I saw them all taking abuse. Yet I never thought that it was ever going to be as bad as it was at some games. It never made me once ever think about not playing football. John Barnes, Terry Connor, Des Walker. They all came through the same sort of environment. All of those kinds of players who played in that era, coming through the 70s and the 80s. Playing football against fans who support teams who have black players, and they love them, but as soon as you get the ball they say all the worst things. You can turn around and say, I'm not going to accept that. What can you do when maybe that person is walking up to you after a game asking you for an autograph, and you're wondering, was he one of those people making a monkey chants at you or another player? You just get on with it. You have to. You don't let anything stand in the way of where you want to go and what you want to be.

I went and watched West Ham a few times with my mates. I was getting spat on and called names while I was watching my local team play. It never, ever once put me off wanting to play football. It's what I'd made my mind up I wanted to be. The only way I wasn't going to be a footballer was if someone told me I wasn't good enough, or if I didn't get selected. People ask if I think being black held me back a bit initially. Look, somewhere along the line, I must have come across through coaching or wherever it was at some point, someone who might have been racist, who may have been going out and saying things when he saw somebody black. I can only share my experience. Did I experience racism from a coach? Never once. I never saw it. It never crossed my mind. However, you might ask, was I looking for it? The answer is, no, I wasn't looking for it, because I was there to play football. I wasn't looking for excuses. And I should add that I never looked upon any racist abuse in my childhood as something that put me into a different category to my friends growing up. They had their own struggles. We were in categories of class – the haves and the have-nots.

I did experience racism from an *opposing* coach. After playing as a striker, and moving to winger, I started moving further back into right-back. So for as long as I was playing in front of crowds throughout my teens, I was close to the touchline. You hear everything from the crowd, and occasionally from the bench. One Saturday morning I was playing for Fulham's youth team at Chadwell Heath, West Ham's old training ground. I was up against Bobby Barnes, a kid superstar. He'd already played first-team football. Another of the young black lads of a generation to look up to. I wasn't going to make it easy for him on the day. I was having a decent game, when Eddie

Baily, the West Ham chief scout (and former Tottenham star) all of a sudden starts having a go at Bobby Barnes.

'Come on, Barnes,' he barks, 'you should be getting past this coon.'

Terry Mancini, who was my youth-team coach, just lost his head. If he'd had any hair he'd have torn it out. John Lyall was the West Ham manager and, like Sir Alex in later years, would always attend the youth games. He made his presence known and gave Eddie Baily the curly finger. I got on with it and I carried on playing, and it was dealt with. Terry Mancini had his say afterwards.

Eddie Baily kept his job. There wasn't a culture then of getting people the sack for something like that. Would I have wanted him to get the sack? Probably not, really. The idea of someone's entire life being turned upside down because of something they've said, a very stupid thing, I don't know – it doesn't seem right.

I played a game for Fulham's first team at Elland Road. I came on as sub. We never lost at Leeds so things were going well for us. I was up against Eddie Gray, the god of Leeds. Eddie dropped the shoulder, I was a little bit late and fouled him. It earned me a chant from the home fans: 'There ain't no black in the Union Jack.' I was only 17. After the game, our manager, Malcolm Macdonald came up to me. Look, I don't know if I really understood what they were saying – I knew they were being racist. I can't remember how I felt but I know I must have seemed emotional, but Malcolm asked me if I was alright. I said I was fine.

'Well,' he goes, 'you've got two choices. You either get on with it or you stop playing, if you can't deal with it.'

So that was as sympathetic as it got. In another industry you'd probably go to HR. But he gave me two choices, and one of them I was never going to take. I went to Leeds on two or three occasions with Fulham. Then again with Queens Park Rangers. In my first season at Manchester United, we played Leeds at Elland Road three times in two weeks because we were drawn against them in both domestic cups. For the first time ever, the Leeds fans called me a red bastard as opposed to a black one. That was my introduction into just how much Leeds United fans hate Manchester United.

Football became much more high profile in the 1990s with Sky and the Premier League. The existence of racism in the game did, too. There was the incident with Eric Cantona at Crystal Palace with the racist fan. Attitudes were changing and stereotypes were becoming outdated. You had popular magazine television programmes like *Soccer AM* and Baddiel and Skinner's shows – lad culture that would carry the casual racist stereotypes, such as the abuse given to Jason Lee, the former Nottingham Forest striker. As time went on there was the Kick It Out campaign and other various approaches to try to address what was going on, and then incidents that would bring it into the news cycle, like Luis Suárez's abuse of Patrice Evra in 2011. Today, social media presents a completely different sort of problem, where anyone can say anything. It's usually someone targeting somebody who has a profile because they want some notoriety for themselves, and it doesn't matter how they get that attention.

Football isn't the owner of racism and it isn't the arbiter. Life is the arena where racism exists. That's where it happens. Yes, football provides a high-profile platform where attitudes can be challenged, but I don't think it can be effectively tackled by T-shirts or badges or taking a knee. I've experienced this myself so I can say it – getting abuse online, in my opinion, doesn't hurt me to the extent that I'd be bothered to track somebody down to find out what I knew anyway, that it was somebody wanting some attention. Of course, there ought to be accountability. Do we need more accountability than the world seeing that person for what they are? What about instead of having that person lose their job, have them go back into their job and face their colleagues. Today we have such a multicultural society that inevitably people are working with people from different cultures, different countries, different religions, different colour of skin. So why not make it uncomfortable by making them go in to face those people after what they've said.

Football can be the same as any workplace for that. Take the example of Enzo Fernández, the Chelsea player who filmed a racist chant about French people while on international duty with Argentina. He got caught up in something. We've got to remember how old he is as well. Footballers are still young men in their own way. When it comes to life skills, they're still quite young, and he's gone and got involved in something that probably they've been doing for quite a while and he's been the one to film it. All of a sudden everyone wants to call him out and say Chelsea should get rid. Money's going to come into it. The biggest thing he's got to do is face the dressing room. Everyone had an opinion on what the black players were going to be saying to him when he got back to Chelsea. Maybe players would just go up to his face and challenge him because they'd socialised with him before, and their opinion of him from the person they know is that he's not racist. They just know he got caught up in something and he'd become a sheep. The education comes in facing those people he knows and sees every day.

The Suárez and Evra event from 2011 was one that disappointed me. It was obvious that Suárez was in the wrong – that part should have been straightforward. But it wasn't. Kenny Dalglish, a legend of the game, backed him, and made the players wear T-shirts in support of Suárez. Supporters were arguing in defence of him over the nuance of what he meant to say, and it caused incredibly hostile atmospheres in the game, which is already the biggest in England. They weren't supporting Suárez on the basis of improving understanding of racism; they were supporting him because the opposing player played for Manchester United. So, while football provides a platform for these things to be addressed in such a public way, it also creates conflict and confrontation that has nothing to do with the actual issue of racism.

My experience of racism has been that – not accounting for obvious individual incidents, and not discounting systemic racism – by and large it was mob mentality caused by ignorance, people following like sheep. It has improved as society has become more multicultural and there has been more education and empathy. The rise of social media means that mob mentality is still there and is maybe even making something of a comeback, but there's now much greater individual accountability and, where that's the case, I do feel and believe that hopefully as we move into a new generation, that greater accountability will mean that racism becomes less of a problem.

Will it ever be eradicated? Sadly, in my opinion, not in a million years. I think that it benefits too many people. People can lobby and politically engineer based on their mobilising, empowering and weaponising racism in whatever manner they choose. People can use racism to create conflict as a means to their own end. As long as doing so can bring them power, or money, there will always be some who want to keep racism alive and thriving.

2

Learning the Hard Way

DISCOVERY IS a funny word. It gives the impression that the thing has never been seen before. You could go really deep about it and think about the archaeologists who find dinosaur bones, but those dinosaurs did previously exist, and they were large enough to not need to be described as a discovery. I may now be old enough to be considered a fossil; I was once one of hundreds of young hopefuls, dreaming of being that player who scored the winning goal in a cup final at Wembley. Without conceit, I was already good enough to play for local sides. A discovery in football does, then, require some effort from the person who hopes to be found. The person who's credited with making the find puts themselves in a favourable position to do so. A scout improves their odds by going to an organised match. So it's not a complete random game of chance – but it does nonetheless take a trained eye to spot talent, or potential, earlier than another scout. That's the distinction of a good scout. Maybe, though, the environment they're in plays a big part; maybe the coaches of the team deserve some credit. I feel like you could say something of everything contributed to Derek Quigley recommending me to

Fulham, considering I was one of three lads from my Romford Juniors team to end up as apprentices at Craven Cottage. We were a good team. I say that because, generally speaking, the number of players we heard about being invited for trials was quite low. Lower still, the number of players you'd hear who would actually sign anywhere.

Derek was a lovely fellow, an Irishman who had a reputation for being everywhere. He told me I should go to Fulham to train. I went home and asked my parents. They said no, it's too far. They had a training facility in Dagenham, only two miles up the road from where I lived. What convinced my mum and dad was probably my persistence. Or stubbornness. I wasn't going to do anything other than play football, and all I wanted to do was try to play as often as I could any given week. They were somewhat encouraged when I was invited to train at Arsenal, because a couple of my mates were there, so we could travel together. But they didn't like the thought of me coming home so late, and I didn't even dare tell them about the near misses I had with the skinheads. Because I was going to football anyway, and there were still a few of my mates who were at Fulham, my parents just accepted that I was enjoying myself. At the age of 14, I signed schoolboy forms, and that meant you were bound to the club for two years. In-between times, I'd often get a lift home, to the relief of my parents. Like the time I was dropped off by George Best.

George was at Fulham at the time. At the risk of sounding even more like a fossil, the mid-70s was a time when football was blessed with an abundance of players with character. They were larger than life. Craven Cottage had become a bit of a magnet for them. There was the high-profile trio of George, Rodney Marsh and Bobby Moore, but with a supporting cast of Viv Busby, John Mitchell, Peter Mellor, Les Strong, it was always a very lively place. Even the manager, Bobby Campbell, was a celebrity of sorts; best friends with the comedian Jimmy Tarbuck, a real presence. I always think there should be more characters in today's football because they're 100 per cent more comfortable financially nowadays. There's more opportunity to laugh when you're that comfortable, rather than being on the edge. Then, you had to work hard to get your money. You had to get to the top to earn your money. Today, players don't really look like they enjoy themselves as much as footballers did back then. Rodney Marsh and George Best played with smiles on their faces.

It was nice to see that, for George in particular, although I was a kid at the time and I'm speaking now with the benefit of hindsight. All the teams that George played for after he left United, well, the media were always going to focus on that team. He had that in the States and he had it at Fulham, although it seemed as though he was enjoying his time there. He played some good football and one of the most famous games of the decade in England was Fulham's home game with Hereford in September 1976, where George and Rodney thrilled the crowd with their skills in a 4-1 win – and then made them laugh when they tried to tackle each other.

George was with his girlfriend Angie at the time, and she lived in Southend, so on one occasion he told me he'd give me a lift. I'm sure it was a Jaguar, and although I can't be 100 per cent sure of my memory, for the purpose of this story I'll refer to it as such. You'll get the point. He dropped me off in a layby opposite my mum's house. The house she still lives in today. A car like that pulls up and suddenly everybody is out having a look. Is it a gangster? Is it the police? My mum twitched the curtain and came outside. I got out of the car, crossed over the road, walked to the house. I thought she was going to give me a clump round the head because she felt that I should have invited him in! He dropped me off. I don't think it meant as much to George as it did to me. To be truthful, at the time it didn't even mean as much to me as it would in later years.

I next saw George in 1991, when I was in the Midland Hotel in Manchester, having just signed for the club. George used to come in there all the time because of Sean McCarthy, who was the general manager of the hotel. George used to come in and he had an entourage with him, including his girlfriend at the time, Mary Shatila. There was one fellow who I knew very well within the group, a man called Phil Black who had a clothes shop in the Exchange Arcade. One night, Phil invited me to come and sit with them.

George used to drink Louis XIV brandy, which came in a beautiful looking bottle. He offered me a drink. I accepted, but I was quite ignorant of brandy at the time, particularly the more expensive brands. I start looking around for the server. George asks what I'm doing, because I'm sure it must have looked odd to him. I said I wanted some coke for the brandy. I barely even managed to finish that sentence before George whipped the bottle from me. He said something to the effect of, 'Don't ever disrespect this brandy again!'

I stayed with him for about an hour and a half nursing that brandy. I was just humbled that a man who'd achieved what he'd achieved, a man regarded by many as the best player to have ever played the game, could remember who I was, and could remember our brief time together at Fulham.

Of course, by then I was 27, and at the time I first met him I was probably barely a teenager. So, now the namedropping is out of the way, back to my days as an apprentice. That was the first step towards the dream of becoming a professional, and it felt like a big accomplishment, but the reality of being a footballer wasn't just training and playing games. When you're seeing the professionals every day, you're kind of in awe of them. At least at that time, you were virtually subservient to them; you had to be, because otherwise you'd be pulled out and you'd be put to task if you weren't.

I was getting up at 6.30am. I used to travel on the train with my mum most of the time because she was going to a place called Charles Street in the city. It was a big area for law firms, and Mum was a traffic warden in the district. Other times I'd travel with the other lads who'd come from Dagenham and Romford. We had to be at the ground by about half-past eight. We had to get the kit out, get the boots; each of us had about six or seven pros to deal with. We had to make sure our bags and theirs got on to the minibus. We didn't have a training ground, we were like cuckoos. We had a place we used called The Bank of England Sports Centre at Roehampton next to

Richmond Park. We couldn't keep anything there, so we had to bring it in a big kind of sack like a postman's bag. We'd carry it in and then get into the changing room, put the kit out and get changed before the pros came in.

My first full-time coach as a youth player at 16 was Terry Mancini. We'd go out and train, and once the pros had finished, our training session would be rounded up then the pros went in take their gear off, and we'd go round and pick up all the sloppy seconds. They'd go and have lunch and we'd hope that something had been left for us. It was like that every day, then we'd get back to the ground by 2 o'clock and get all the stuff out of the bags, take the kit into the washroom and then go to the boot room to get the mud off everyone's boots. Once a week we had to clean the ground. The worst bit was when there was a match on. We used to hate Fridays before games, because all the pros would come in, train at the ground and they'd be gone by 12 o'clock. We'd have to go all the way around the ground to the Riverside Stand and clean out the toilets. Clean *everything*. On Fridays we weren't getting home until 6 or 7pm, and I was up on a Saturday morning 6 or 7am for the game kicking off at 11. You'd play in the game, rush back over Putney Bridge to get back to Craven Cottage to make sure the boots for the pros were perfect, down to the stripes looking gleaming.

It was a hard gig to do that, and there were big punishments like, for example, towel whippings, or the time I got boot-polished. If you want to know what that is, then you don't need to extend your imagination too far. You're held down, someone goes into the boot room, brings out the polish and rubs it all over you. I was darker than I am now. I was sitting in a train, it was about 35 or 36 stops from Putney Bridge to Elm Park. You can't just wash the wax off. It took about two days. I couldn't sleep in the bed. I had to sit up on old towels on a chair.

That rite of passage seemed to change by the time I became a pro at 18 in 1982. The young apprentices still showed respect, but you weren't asking for it … maybe it's because of what we'd been through. Some people dealt with it better than others. Some people moaned about it. Tony Gale tells me stories about when he was an apprentice in the years before I was on the scene.

I can say, honestly, that I felt that I dealt with it well. I felt it was a good education for me, and it prepared me to have resilience. Today, there's none of that, and some might say thankfully so; clearly, some of it was beyond the pale, but, for example, there's nothing wrong with being a boot boy. Today, kids in their mid-teens are getting boot *deals*. I think if you're a parent with your kid in an academy, you'd want them to have a good solid base to build from and that comes from working *for* people, and understanding that's the case. So you have to be prepared for that person demanding more from you, being able to demand hard work without someone calling it bullying if someone's telling them they're not working hard enough. I've seen it; I've seen coaches scream at someone to run faster in a game, or someone tell a player, 'You ain't working hard enough,' and I've seen the response that it's a form of bullying. You don't like it, especially if it's in front of other people when you're being questioned or you're being criticised. It hurts. But it's up to you to go and prove that person wrong. Go out there and go and do that, and show you're not slacking; go and prove that you can give more. Okay, you shouldn't really have to ask but we've all had our moments where we've had those days where we're not feeling right and we're trying to get away with it.

Our game would be better served if we were to go back to some form of apprenticeship to understand life and being a footballer. You suddenly can't decide I'm going to be a watchmaker and straight away you're working with Rolexes; you have to go through life learning. You can't decide I'm going to be a car mechanic and then start working on the engine of a Lamborghini.

It seems as though some parents are accepting and happy that their kids are going straight into something; everything is clean, they can just go into work and they're given everything, nice tracksuits, they get sponsored, they get their boots, and then they get the hump when their manager has a go at them and criticises them. Then they want to come out on social media and call people out. I'd want my kids to have a bit of a backbone about them and that backbone is gained by going into the dressing room, picking up kit, going around cleaning boots – just a little bit of work to understand when they get there, what's behind them, what it takes. A little bit of understanding.

The point about that is that it builds resilience and it builds character. Resilience is how you bounce back from a setback, so there has to *be* a setback, even if that setback is that your performance didn't meet the expectation of the coach, which is generally the first criticism a player gets. You can't have a kid to go into that environment and already know what resilience is, to know what hard work is, because you're then saying it has to be inherently built into them. It's impossible, and unfair, to expect that a kid ought to automatically know without needing to be told. It's unrealistic. That's what education is.

Okay, I'm talking about at a teenage level, but it carries on into the senior game. It's a development of personality. It's a test of character. Will a player sulk or will they turn around and do something about it? Sir Alex was great at doing that – sometimes I saw some things in the dressing room where he'd go after a player to test what he was made of. I'd see him after, and he'd maybe say sarcastically, 'There you go, I was right, I knew you could do it, I told you you could do it.' But he'd be big enough to do that, and he was great at doing it. The timing was always immaculate, and it always served a purpose. Jim Smith was very, very much like that in a way that's now considered to be old-fashioned. I think there's a culture of feeling that conditions are better today and, because we didn't have it, the next generation should, and what we did have, the next generation shouldn't. So we didn't have agents. Today they do. So we got criticism. Today you won't, because the agent will be asking questions or making demands. You're not allowing an individual to have their own grounding.

You're also at the risk of taking away their individuality, to bring it back to the point I was speaking about earlier. The improvisation you used to see everywhere has been replaced by a desire to register good numbers. Don't do anything too risky. You'll affect your stats. I don't think we're a million miles away from it. Kids still grow up wearing No.7 and No.10, wanting to be Ronaldo or Messi. They do that because they see them doing exceptional things. That's how you fall in love with the game. And, fortunately for my own education, that's how I recall my early education at a professional level, though my No.7 was Best and No.10 was Marsh.

By the time I was at Fulham I wasn't under any illusion that I was going to be a Best or Marsh. The most optimistic comments made about me when I was playing as a right-winger for Romford Juniors or Pegasus, another of my junior teams, was 'boot it over the top and Paul Parker's going to run and shoot'. Note the deliberate turn of phrase. Not Paul Parker's going to *score*. Because even Paul Parker sometimes didn't know what was going to happen next.

I went to Romford with a lad called Dean Coney and he was probably the best forward around in the Essex district. He was a kid superstar. To be frank, it wasn't just Dean, there were other players who were better forwards than me. Because I was right-footed, the next natural place to try me was at right-back, because I was quick and tenacious, and, let's face it, I was also little. I wasn't afraid to tackle and I was good at cleaning things up. I was also distinctive for another reason – I was the only black kid in my team. The other sides in the league had a lot of black of players, so particularly in the East London games I'd get stick from them or their parents, asking me why I was playing in a team of white men, or why I talked the way I did.

It was tough. I laughed it off, initially, but it did get at me. Couldn't show it, though. So it becomes part of the armoury you build around yourself. As a player. As a person.

From memory, most of the wingers I came up against were black lads. Inner London kids. Tons of aggression, no great discipline. They'd see me and think I was an easy touch. They'd think again after playing against me. I was always fighting back. By the time I was 16 or 17, all those players had disappeared. There was one notable difference, a lad called Bobby Barnes, who, of course, was a very special case.

I quickly came to love defending. The *art* of defending. I can't remember scoring goals too often but I can remember the feeling when you make a big tackle. A big block tackle. A slide-tackle. Hearing one of your mates screaming at you that you've done something brilliant. These days you see it go that extra mile – players doing high-fives, giving back-slaps. To borrow a phrase from a former team-mate: that was my job. It was expected of me. Still, there was nothing like that feeling of when you executed a tackle so perfectly that it drew a reaction.

One of the first things that comes to mind is a tackle at Old Trafford in front of the Stretford End – but playing for QPR, not United, in the famous FA Cup trilogy of early 1989. Lee Sharpe was playing left-back and he was about to accelerate, so I knew I had to make a big challenge. We both fearlessly went in and I can still remember the noise of the ball as we both made contact with it, with all of our might. *Bang*. It startled both of us for a second; I think he thought the same thing as me, that we'd burst the ball. I got a pat on the back from Alan

McDonald – and a song from the Stretford End, who were less appreciative.

They were more receptive on a similar occasion, against Arsenal in March 1993. I'm not quite sure if it was Paul Merson or Ian Wright – an easy pair to confuse, I'm sure you'll agree – but one of them was just about to shoot when I stole in from right-back and just about got my right foot across to block it. I'd say it was an almost guaranteed goal, but we did have big Peter Schmeichel in goal, so … You rarely see a defender who loves defending in that way in the modern game. You rarely see tackles like the one I went in on with Sharpey – now both players would scream, roll around and probably be startled by the noise the ball made.

I was fortunate enough to score a couple of times in my career, so the feeling isn't completely alien to me. And, like I said, the dream when you're a kid is scoring in the cup final. But there does come a moment where that dream of becoming a footballer matures into some form of realisation. I can be a footballer, in this position. I'm accomplished in this area. In that time of repositioning, I was facing either those questions about my choices as a black player in a majority-white team or just straightforward racism from opponents. Dagenham and Barking as a district had the biggest National Front following in the Greater London boroughs. Pubs would have flags outside. There was a pub called the Church Elm in Dagenham that had a massive St George's flag with National Front written across the front of it. It was there for ages. So I had to deal with that, and when I played well I didn't feel comfortable being singled out. I felt as though they were making a fuss because I was distinctive, and I didn't want that. I didn't want a pat on the head, a pat on the back. It accentuated the difference. I felt as though it was a special effort to let me know that they'd noticed I'd done well. It probably wasn't – it could well have been a natural reaction to how well I was playing. But when so much is made of your difference, your natural reaction is to push against that.

It does create a complex. I knew I had to play well every single game because if things weren't going right, I'd be the first player off. Okay, you might say when you're losing a game and chasing a result that you'll bring off the right-back. But there was the bigger picture, for me, and I knew it wasn't just about being brought off, it was about my chances of making it at all. Being brought off is only one step away from being left out. I knew I'd be the easiest one to take off; so it made me all the more determined that it wouldn't happen to me.

The vindication I had of my ability was in the progress I made, getting to Fulham, being offered schoolboy terms. I quickly discovered, though, that thinking you've made it is a misapprehension. That requirement for you to prove yourself, or the feeling that there's something about you that somebody else is unconvinced about, never really goes away. It didn't help that I was about 5ft 4in. Terry Mancini, the youth-team coach at Fulham, was very, very sceptical of me because of my size. Because of that, in my first year as a schoolboy I rarely got games at the weekend. I'd be on the side, watching. I was sent to the old St Stephen's Hospital in Westminster to go and get a bone check, an X-ray to see how tall I was going to be. They said I'd be about 5ft 8in (I wonder if I can go back and get a bit of compensation, because I only got to five seven!).

I was short and there was nothing on me. I wasn't carrying any muscle bulk. I was like a whippet. Obviously there was always that worry about me getting bashed about a bit by these big kids, especially when you played some of the teams like Millwall. Their youth team included lads who'd already played a fair number of games in the first team. Kevin O'Callaghan, Paul Roberts, Dave Martin, Dean Horrocks, all these players who played in the Millwall side and won the Youth Cup in 1979. You can't really prove yourself without being given the opportunity – but I did, and really, considering the circumstances, it's made me think that I went through all of that in such a short space of time and made my professional debut at 17.

Size mattered in football, especially at that time. I still don't know what convinced Terry to give me a chance. Maybe it was my attitude in waiting without complaining. Maybe I'd shown some persistence. Maybe it was just a gut feeling. We had a decent youth team. We were competitive – we were never likely to win the FA Youth Cup, or any regional cup for that matter, but we were committed and we played for each other. There was certainly a deeper long-term strategy at play, because I think nine of us went on to play together in the first team. The club had speculated financially and Ernie Clay eventually pulled out as chairman, so there was also a necessity for Fulham to bring players into the senior side.

We were doing quite well in the 80s, but when we missed out on promotion to the First Division in 1983, it sent us more backwards than really it ought to have. We lost a lot of good players, like Gerry Payton, Tony Gale, Gordon Davies and Ray Houghton, in a short space of time, and that youth team made up the majority of the first team, so much so that I was made captain by the age of 21. Missing out on promotion hurt and, really, I think the team we had did well to compete for a couple of seasons in the Second Division. Financially, it couldn't continue, and eventually we were relegated back to the Third Division.

3

Ups and Downs at Fulham

I JUMPED ahead, didn't I? Let me talk a little more about Fulham, starting with the moment I signed my professional contract. Or, the moment I became a professional footballer, because when I broke into the team at 17 I was still an apprentice, earning apprentice money – £16 a week, with a win bonus of somewhere between £60 and £80. When the club offered you a contract, there was no negotiation, you took what you were given.

Bobby Campbell had left as manager and Malcolm Macdonald, the distinctive former centre-forward who scored tons of goals for Newcastle and Arsenal, and had started at Fulham, was now in charge. He was only 30, having retired early. He signed me as a professional. I recall the scene, being invited to go and see him, and it was very typical early 80s, sitting behind his desk, smoking a big thick cigar. He'd talk but not look you in the eye. This is what we're giving you, he said in a husky voice. One of the great characters of the last decade. Of course, you just accepted it. No big picture with your parents, no grand ceremony. You're a professional now. Get on with your job.

You were a professional, but still only a junior professional. The promotion meant I no longer had to clean boots. The dirty kit? Sweeping the dressing room? Still doing those. Having waited for a chance at reserve-team level, though, I only had to play nine times before I was called up by Malcolm to make my professional debut against Reading at home in April 1981. I was told by Malcolm to man-mark Kerry Dixon, all six foot of him. That was the Third Division. I think most of the Reading team were that size. It was eerie – it was daunting. We lost the game.

I played a few more games the following season, when we were promoted to the Second Division. Things were going right. There were some good players in the first team and the continuity and togetherness of the young group I was a part of made for a decent blend. Malcolm was a good man-manager but was helped by Roger Thompson and George Armstrong. Roger and Malcolm knew each other at Arsenal, and I'd say Roger was probably the brains of the operation. George was probably the fittest man I've ever known. All he wanted to do was stomach exercises all day. I think all of us have had hernia operations and it was probably because of that. Ray Harford came in as youth-team coach, with Terry moving to the reserve team. The combinations through the club were working well together and promotion was secured with a 1-1 draw against Lincoln. The late Roger Brown scored the goal and was pictured in an iconic pose, smoking a cigar in celebration.

He was a lovely man, Roger, and he made such a big difference. He wasn't the greatest with a football at his feet, but no one was ever going to beat him in the air. He was so aggressive, he was frightening on the football pitch, and he was unafraid to stick his head anywhere. But off the pitch he was such a humble man. Roger was the right-sided centre-half, so the man at the side of me, and on his left was Tony Gale.

Promotion to the Second Division enabled us to attract a higher calibre of player. Amazingly, Ray Houghton, still only 20, came on a free transfer from West Ham. And I remember we were training in Bishops Park and Malcolm Macdonald brought him across to join in with us. We were blown away with him. Ray was brilliant and helped to bring the best out of Gordon Davies, who was a great goalscorer for the level we needed.

We had a great season and on the final day of the campaign we were playing at Derby with a chance of promotion. We had to win and hope that Leicester, who were also battling to go up, didn't win against Burnley. It was intimidating at the Baseball Ground; there would be no love lost between themselves and Leicester, so maybe the atmosphere was something to do with that, but it was all quite tense. I was on the bench. We didn't play well. We fell behind. We didn't deserve anything from the game. Towards the end, supporters started to get closer to the pitch, and I remember being surprised that they wanted to run on it at all, considering the state of the surface. It was just mud, it hadn't recovered from the winter. One of our players, Jeff Hopkins, took all of our throw-ins, and every time he got the ball he was taking punches and kicks from fans around the side. It got worse as the game went on. As I recall it, the referee blew his whistle, and I don't think it was to stop the game. It was for some incident similar to the one happening with Jeff. I don't think the fans were even really watching the game in the end. They were jostling for positions, maybe looking to get themselves out of chairs. They heard a whistle and bang, they ran across the pitch. Jeff Hopkins got absolutely battered, taking whacks everywhere.

And he was right on the far side. The referee didn't even say anything. He could have turned around – referees of today would say something and then get everyone into an area and bang, you're off. But at that time, football was different. It wasn't a safety-first sport as such. When Jeff finally got into the dressing room, he was absolutely emotionally in bits. And Jeff was a tough, tough man, by the way. No fear about him. But that was an extreme situation. Myself, I'd jumped off of the bench, because the benches were quite long, and I didn't want to get trapped by the Derby fans in front of me. I went to run down the tunnel and was attacked by the mascot ram! The ram hit me on my thighs, with sharp horns, and bowled me over. People were trying to run past the tunnel and I'm trying to get off the floor after the ram had taken me out.

Malcolm was absolutely fuming that the game had ended early and he tried to really push for a replay but they were never going to give anything. They couldn't have done that. They were scared of setting a precedent over something like that, because it's an easy thing for people to go and do to change an outcome of a game.

The result did cost us, though. Momentum is such a strong thing in football, in a game, over a season, over a course of a few years. Stories of success are littered with those sliding doors moments and people like to fantasise about what might have happened, if things didn't go right. For example, Mark Robins scoring in 1990 when Alex Ferguson seemed close to losing his job as Man Utd manager. United went on to have this tremendous era, which I was honoured to be a part of, but people like to throw in the hypothetical. What if Mark hadn't scored? Well, Fulham in 1983 was an example of what happens when it doesn't work out. The next three years saw unbelievable change, most of it backwards.

There was one last hurrah from that period and that was when we drew Liverpool in the following season's League Cup. At the time, this was probably Liverpool's greatest-ever team, with Dalglish, Rush, Souness and Hansen. They'd go on to win the league, European Cup and the League Cup, but we gave them a good scare. It was also the tie that really launched my career. Malcolm decided to leave out Roger and play me alongside Tony Gale, a decision that raised eyebrows, for obvious reasons. My reaction, on instinct, was to feel sorry for Roger. I didn't feel comfortable taking his place. We fought and got a draw, to earn a replay at Anfield. When I was named in Roger's place again, once more I thought more about him at first than I did the job at hand. I'd actually accepted that I'd be going to Anfield and seeing this incredible ground in person, at a time when football wasn't on the television multiple times a week, and when it was on, invariably it was Liverpool playing in Europe.

But leading up to the game, all the work was being done with me playing at centre-half. Roger Brown was absolutely fuming and was letting it be known as well, which made it even more difficult. I had to concentrate, though; Ian Rush, who I'd be marking again, was a formidable opponent. I sussed out quite early that Rush had this way of playing, in that he tried to talk to me. He talked, talked, talked, and then bang, he was gone. The first time he did it, I reacted well, and luckily enough I was able to get there and make a challenge. And after that, I just ignored what he was trying to do. There was 100 per cent no malice in his game, it was just a distraction technique, and he never, ever switched off. Every now and then I couldn't help but smile at how much he was going on, but when I look back at those games I know it was the first time I had to concentrate as much as that.

We somehow got a draw at Anfield. It took everything – we pushed ourselves to more than our limits. I went into a challenge with Craig Johnston and I knew instantly it was a bad one. I could feel it. Souness came over. He said, 'Oh, don't look down at that.' So obviously I did … and I threw up. It was a knee ligament injury that kept me out of the third game between us. The lads took it to extra time. Souness scored the decisive goal in the 114th minute. It was an epic run of games. You don't get second replays today. In the League Cup you don't get any. One bite of the cherry. We got three. We didn't let ourselves down. It was hard work, but we weren't hanging on, it wasn't backs-to-the-wall stuff.

There was a journalist called Steve Stammers, who was writing for the *Daily Star*. After those games he did a profile on me, and interviewed me for it. He asked if there was anything else I'd wanted to be. I told him that I wanted to be a footballer but the careers advisor at school had said only a one in a million make it. I wasn't good at maths, but I knew the population was about 45 to 50 million people living in the UK. Still, Steve's headline for the piece was 'One in a million'. I kept seeing him around. I got involved with England, for the youth team, the U21s, and he was always there. It turned out that we lived close to each other, so he'd give me lifts to and from the airport. He told the worst jokes in the world, but you felt obliged to laugh. Sadly, he passed away during lockdown, but I have to say that it was his attention to highlight me that gave me a bigger profile.

Things were getting better for me but getting worse for Fulham. I was improving; the club was struggling. Liverpool, having seen me close up, made an offer for me. My problem was that the chairman liked me. Ernie Clay was a proper, proud Yorkshireman, and he'd always make a beeline for me whenever he saw me. He didn't really want to let me go. Liverpool offered and he asked for a little more. Liverpool said they wouldn't pay it because I was 'just potential'. It didn't work out. At the time, Liverpool signed a lot of younger players and they never got going. You didn't see them in the first team. They played reserve-team football for ages and the usual 11 or 12 players played every week.

We had a poor run of form but stabilised to stay up; it wasn't enough for Malcolm to keep his job. He left, so did some of our better players, and all of a sudden the lads who'd come through the youth system into the first team to supplement the good experience and quality we had were now on our own. We had our moments, but we weren't experienced or robust enough. It was a very difficult league. We brought Tony Sealy in from Crystal Palace, and he did well, but it's always a very difficult thing to do to turn around a situation rather than build upon it. We lost key players at the wrong time, and everything that had been built up was just disappearing. It just got really, really difficult. As much as you try to be as honest as possible, you just know it isn't going to work. So, in my own mind, with the club I'd been with from the age of 11, I knew that my time was up.

Ray Harford came in as manager. He was a great youth-team coach, someone I respected hugely, someone who had a big impact on my career. I spoke to him all the time, years after I left the club. But it wasn't working out for him. Ray Lewington then took over. We'd all played with him. That didn't work, either. We had a return to Anfield in another League Cup match. This time we were beaten 10-0. It was a different Fulham. We were relegated back into the Third Division.

Ernie left as chairman. David Bulstrode, a man with a property background, took over. Jimmy Hill came in with his consortium, offering to take over the club, and he took us all down to his house on the south coast. He was chatting to everyone. Everyone except me. Spent ages talking to them all. Went around them all. Maybe I shouldn't have really been that bothered, but I did take it a bit personally. He had this practice net for golf shots in his back garden. I got a club and took a swing at a ball – without thinking. I don't think Gary Player would have been pleased. Jimmy wasn't. I hit it straight into the opposite direction, into his patio doors. I made my own way home. I could say Jimmy didn't put across in any way that he wanted me to stay but, equally, I was now wanting to leave. So was Dean Coney. Bulstrode liked us both, and wanted to look after us. He gave me a big company car, an Audi. It was so big I thought I might need a booster cushion and blocks for my feet. Bulstrode started talking about a merger of Fulham and QPR, which didn't go down well with fans of either club. Fulham Park Rangers. Bulstrode eventually went to Loftus Road as chairman and at the same time a deal was proposed for me and Dean to go there too. I didn't really have a say in it. It was put to us that Fulham needed the money to survive. If that was to happen today, any player in their right mind would say, well, who else wants me? I was joining a great club in QPR; they'd had some great times in the 1970s with Gordon Jago, Dave Sexton, then later with Terry Venables, and Jim Smith was now the manager. But I was going there not knowing whether I was even wanted by the manager or whether I'd been a pawn in some bigger game.

4

The Top Tier with QPR

IF FULHAM had enjoyed a reputation in the 1970s as a glamour London club, then QPR were well-deserving of theirs as a serious outfit throughout the decade. Gordon Jago had built a good young team and then Dave Sexton had taken them to second place in the First Division in 1976; he did so well at Loftus Road that he was hired by Manchester United. They'd been relegated after that, but had gone back up to the top flight under Terry Venables. A fifth-placed finish under Terry saw him headhunted by Barcelona, and QPR struggled under Alan Mullery and Frank Sibley before Jim Smith came in to stabilise things.

By the time Dean and I made the move, talk of a merger between QPR and Fulham was pretty much dead in the water. I was happy in a sense that I was familiar with this part of the world and obviously it was a move to the First Division. Supporters were happy that they'd got their way and could still follow their own clubs. Considering the recent successes of both of them, you can understand why the fans were fiercely against it. In some ways David Bulstrode was ahead of his time;

I remember they were talking about converting some of Craven Cottage into apartments, but then it came to be a conversation about just moving the whole operation to Loftus Road and using the space at Fulham for a residential development. In football, you have periods where supporters don't believe their voice is being heard, but sometimes when the noise is loud enough, it can't be ignored. QPR fans would protest on the pitch and they made their point. I don't think I was ever convinced that it could work. It rarely does, and the difficult history of MK Dons tells us why, because football clubs are part of the community and they're not franchises.

Business in football always seems to be a process of pushing it until there's either resistance or it reaches a point of no return. Ticket prices rise, bigger clubs will try to convert regular seats into corporate tickets, they'll do what they can to get as much money as possible and make it difficult for a supporter with a season ticket to have much say. The greatest modern success supporters have had against the 'system' was the coming together to protest against the European Super League. There's no denying that the protests did spook the clubs into publishing statements saying they were going to withdraw from it. In that case, however, I think it was just a case of kicking the can down the road. It wasn't the right time. It feels inevitable. UEFA's response was to expand the Champions League and Europa League. It's far, far too much. A convoluted group stage led to saturation of games and a loss of interest, for me, personally. Decent sides are playing way above their levels, conceding a load of goals. It's not interesting because it's not competitive.

The Champions League was supposed to be about the elite. It was already pushing that when second-placed teams were allowed to enter, and now it's been pushed to the extent where there are two leagues, a domestic and a European league, and it won't be long until the Super League as a topic is reintroduced.

On that topic of saturation of games, and the globalisation of the Premier League, we now have a situation where high-profile foreign players are complaining about the number of games played in England, and, for a time in 2024, there were rumours of a possible strike. Could you imagine an Englishman playing abroad in any other country, in Italy, Spain or Germany saying, 'I'm going on strike. We're playing too many games!' That player would be happily invited to return to England. We don't – we indulge it and accept it because it's, for example, a Spanish player of notoriety. They want to listen to him and then people are starting to agree with him, and it sets a wheel in motion for huge changes in English football. How many more do we need? The League Cup has already been run ragged over the last generation, and we're talking about one of the country's major cup competitions. This is our passion, our love, our heritage. As much as I want to think that the supporters will eventually win out, I think this has always been a long game for some of the big clubs, for the Premier League and for UEFA too. The issue looks as though it's been moved into the future but the bodies are effectively preparing their position of strength in order to exploit the situation for the maximum amount of money possible. It impacts the credibility of the output. It already has. You can say the stakes are higher financially, the players are more athletic, the surfaces are pristine and the facilities have never been better, but it's almost universally accepted that the quality of the sport, from an individual or watchability viewpoint, has significantly regressed.

Players are accused of being mercenaries. And rightly so, in some circumstances. In others, clubs are quick to view players as dispensable. It can be a case of use or be used. I still love Fulham, but I admit that the circumstances in which I left were not ideal. Endings are rarely amicable, and nobody wants to feel as though they're not wanted. I can't lie though; I can't say I wasn't ambitious, that I'd not already started to have the feeling of wanting to move on and test myself at a higher level.

I'd like to sit here and say that I never let my team-mates down, I didn't let the club down. I don't think I did. I made it known I was ready to leave if the right offer came, but I didn't agitate to move. Things began to escalate; seeing team-mates leave, being part of a struggle, the financial difficulty of the club. And, admittedly, towards the end, I confess that I was probably part of the group who pushed the ex-team-mates bit a little too far with Ray Lewington and it made life harder for him. I'm not saying we undermined him but we perhaps didn't show the respect we should have done, and I was immediately regretful of that.

So I can say, with honesty, that my complaint was more to do about not having a choice of where to go. Would I have gone and joined a team in the Second Division? Well, this is with hindsight of not having the choice and going straight into the top league, but I think I'd have probably stayed at Fulham.

So, there were similarities between them and QPR – both had become fairly fashionable over the prior 15 years or so, but it should be said that QPR had that track record of top-flight success. There was something special about the bragging rights of being the top club in London. Geography plays a part, too; Chelsea, being situated where they are in the West End, were always seen as the glamour club of the capital, but QPR being in close proximity and then doing as well as they had in recent years had made them a serious contender for that title.

In the season when we missed out on promotion to the top flight with Fulham, QPR finished the Second Division as champions. The football they played and the players they had … it was special. They also stood out because of the plastic pitch at Loftus Road. You played on it as a visitor and it took you by surprise, but the more you got used to it, playing on it every other week and training on it, the better it got. I know some have complained about injuries picked up, the damage it did to joints, but I can only speak from my experience and say that I didn't encounter any of that. My main injury when I was there was a knee injury picked up in a challenge with the Southampton goalkeeper in a Zenith Data Cup game.

When I first got there I had to learn about the habits of the pitch. The bounce in dry weather and wet weather. You have to learn about how to how to approach the ball, when to control and when to just clear your lines. When and when not to gamble. Whether to chase the ball or when not to bother.

Anything hit high and with pace would always run so fast that it would go out for a goal kick. If you wanted to play a good attacking pass, you had to basically clip it, or chip it with a bit of backspin on it, if you wanted to stand a chance. The one thing it does is really sharpen your focus on your control of the ball. That's no bad thing for a footballer who's trying to find his feet in the First Division.

Also not a bad thing for a player who was told on his arrival, 'You're a good defender, but you can't fucking pass the ball, so give it to someone who can.' Those words of wisdom were imparted by Peter Shreeves, the assistant to Jim Smith. Okay, sounds harsh, but I accepted it. If I was being truthful with myself, I'd coasted at Fulham; not in terms of taking it easy with my performance, but I was already earning rave reviews, and when that's the case you don't naturally consider what you need to do to improve. That wasn't the case in the First Division.

I knew that I'd need to step up. It was difficult, but I was just thrown in at the deep end, and my first concern was whether or not Jim Smith even wanted me, or if it had just been a part of the proposed merger. There was already a very good right-back in Warren Neill, and I just couldn't see myself playing there. Jim, though, had decided to go to three at the back, which would be me, Terry Fenwick and Alan McDonald. Me and Macca were man-markers, and Fen was a sweeper. Fen was a great sweeper, great centre-half, but one hell of a nasty bastard. Nasty, but very clever with how he'd do it. He was a Terry Venables lieutenant in the way he played, on and off the pitch, an organiser, a bit like Bryan Robson in his own way. It felt like he was the leader of the team, protecting you in your position. He was the one ushering you to get closer, to drop off, he'd come in and help you and tell you to get in position. He made life easy.

Easier, at least. One of my first big challenges at QPR came against Everton at home, in only my third home game for the club, in September. I was man-marking Graeme Sharp. Graeme was going absolutely mad; he didn't like the way I was marking him. He'd taken a look at me and probably just thought, *Who's this skinny kid they've put up against me?* I was 23 years of age but there still wasn't a lot about me. But I'd been battered and bruised in the Third Division against players like Billy Whitehurst, so the likes of a Graeme Sharp didn't really bother me. I already knew I'd need to over-compensate so I was outjumping him in a lot of cases. I nicked in front of him one time by physically nudging him, but that was enough for him, and he said a few words to me. Not very happy ones. Thankfully enough, Howard Kendall took him off, but life in the top division was all about one quality player after another. He brought on Adrian Heath, a player who was a similar size to me, but broader than me, and I think he caused me more problems because he was always going to be more of a threat to run behind.

Despite this, I relished the challenge. In fact I didn't have that much fear in that first season because I felt I had so much to gain and not so much to lose. It helped that we had a strong start to the season. We defeated Everton and in our next home game Gary Bannister scored a hat-trick to help us defeat Chelsea. We were top of the league, six wins from seven, five clean sheets in there too. It was an incredible time, more so for the club and the fans because they were really enjoying it. I think that common sense was still being held there – I think they were just enjoying the moment. You start a season full of optimism and the sun is shining. As the weeks went on, and we were winning, the games developed an edge, and you grow to love that as a professional.

Then we went to Anfield, and we were taught a bit of a lesson. We held our own for a while but quality told. They had one of the very best players in Europe at the time, John Barnes, and it was extremely tough to play against him. We lost 4-0. I wouldn't say it was a 4-0 sort of game, as I think we did ourselves justice in the way we played, and responded to the goals, but it does bring you down to earth and the realism comes into it. You can tell the difference between a team who can do well and a team that's competing seriously for the title. We had a great system. Liverpool, though, had runners and workers everywhere. Fen, normally so good at organisation, was being dragged about everywhere because they had brilliant movement and no static midfield. They didn't take us for granted. At Fulham, maybe we caught them out a couple of times, and maybe they were a little more relaxed. In this game, they saw our start to the season and took us seriously. Everything was clinical.

Later on in my career, at United, we'd come up against teams like the QPR team I was in at the start of a season.

They'd start the season well and come to Old Trafford on a high, thinking and feeling they've got nothing to lose. They're in good spirits and even if it goes wrong it doesn't matter. You don't usually come up against that fearlessness, and it can be unsettling. You have to be better, you have to concentrate, you have to play well yourself, and you have to take your chances and put them to bed. You can get pulled into an entertaining game but the difference has to be how clinical you are when it matters. Liverpool were.

The strength of any good team, and manager, is how you respond to something like that. Jim Smith was a man who commanded respect. I called him Mr Smith when I first met him to sign for the club, and then naturally I took to calling him boss or gaffer as the other lads did. He was a proper manager. He had clear ideas, he knew what he wanted from his team when it came to coaching and he knew that in Peter Shreeves he had the perfect assistant to help him articulate it. They worked incredibly well together. Sometimes the boss would swear at us and come out and stop the training, he'd have his clipboard in front of him and then Peter would come in with a schoolboy grin on his face when the boss was behind him. 'Lads, let's just get on and do what the boss wants, I know what he wants. He just couldn't find it on his clipboard. He's got too much fucking paper on there!'

Jim and Peter always had a way of lifting the mood, but they were honest with it, and without question that helped the team spirit at the club. In one game, we'd been playing poorly in the first half, so, at the break, Jim comes in and he's going ballistic. Alan McDonald is the target of his anger. Jim had a vein in the middle of his head that would stand out when he was angry, and whenever you saw that as a player you knew it this was going to be heavy. He was livid. Having a right go. Only problem was … no response from Alan, because he was nowhere to be seen. The QPR changing rooms are quite small. You go through a tight tunnel and if you need the toilet, you pass the changing room. That's where Macca was. After a while cursing him, Jim realises he's not there. 'I know where he is!' We hear him storm out in to the toilet. 'Put that fucking cigarette out and get in here!'

Macca used to have a cigarette and a lighter or matches underneath the U-bend in the toilet and he always went and had a cigarette at half-time. It was a custom that I never heard of prior to being at Loftus Road. I knew footballers smoked, but I never knew a player would have a crafty one at half-time. Macca comes in and he goes, 'I already heard you. You're this, you're that, I'm not even in the fucking room and all you can do is say my name.'

Shreeves cut the tension. 'Just come in Macca. You're back now. You're stinking like you've just come out of a working-man's club. Just go out there in the second half and if you've got a problem with the boss sort it out after.' It wasn't spoken about after. Done and dusted, forgotten. I always say Jim is alongside Sir Bobby and Sir Alex in my top three managers. They were incredible in their own different ways.

Jim started played me as a man-marker and sweeper, even in a back four. These were the sort of things that went against the norm, but he just gave you belief that you could do it. He could absolutely slaughter you, but he'd just give you a little smile and say 'go out there and prove me wrong'. It was an incredibly effective strategy with older players and he did it with so many players in that team. When I look at those players I played with at QPR, and how we were working together, it was just a shame that it ended when it did, because of an offer Jim couldn't turn down.

The confidence I developed to play a natural way, to add skills to my range of abilities and to feel that I could express them – that's a strange thing to say for a defender, especially one not renowned for creative ability, but there's something to be said in helping a player understand their own role and importance. I felt at home the moment I got there. From the outside, Terry Fenwick had seemed like the main man, considering his reputation at Crystal Palace and what he'd done at the World Cup in 1986. As soon as I got to Loftus Road, it was noticeable to see the close relationship he and Jim had. But then Jim treated me exactly the same, like I was one of his main players, like it had always been that way. And I felt *comfortable* in that skin. I probably didn't have any right to. I was a kid coming from the Third Division. Yet there I was, feeling like a key player in a top First Division side.

Jim was a social manager. He'd always be with the players. On the coach after a game, he'd be with the players having a laugh and a joke, smoking his cigar. You were left with the impression that he cared. So much so that I still believe that Jim Smith played a part in me going to United. That's jumping ahead.

Anfield had been a harsh lesson but we had a really strong season. We finished fifth – top of the London clubs, and with a great record against them all head-to-head. We played confidently in all of those games, too. It was not like at Fulham, where you were usually the underdogs. Maybe we still were but that wasn't in our attitude. We were unbeaten against Chelsea, Arsenal and Spurs in the season. Beating Spurs at Loftus Road was a very special occasion for me. It was a hell of an atmosphere. It is most times in any big game of any description at Loftus Road. We had just under 15,000 there, but that could have been 35,000 or 45,000 going by the noise they were making. Obviously, it was special to the club to have beaten Chelsea earlier in the season, but being aware of the rivalry and being a part of it are two different things, and that probably came so early that I couldn't fully appreciate it. The Spurs win was special to me.

When we won at Derby the following week, it was a very different feeling to my last visit. That time there had been the heartache of missing out on promotion and I always associated that with the moment it turned around at Fulham. To go there and win comfortably, and to go third in the top flight, was a very special feeling. That would have been enough to qualify for Europe; however, English clubs were still banned from European competitions after Heysel, and in the end we finished fifth, as I said.

So there was no continental experience with QPR but I did play in the President's Cup, a pre-season tournament in South Korea, which was against a Soviet Union XI, the United

States national team and a Nigerian team called Iwuanyanwu Nationale. On that trip I was sharing a room with Warren Neill and Mark Dennis. Mark Dennis was sleeping on the floor, and you were always worried in a room with Mark Dennis. You didn't want to leave him there because you didn't know where your mattress would be when you came back. My memories of the country are vague. I was sent off against the Nigerian side in the first game. It was my first-ever red card. I made a tackle, their lad took offence to it, we exchanged a few words and he spat at me. I was holding the ball, so I flung it right at his face. They wanted me banned for the rest of the tournament so I had to go and plead my case with Jim Smith to be able to play again. It was reduced to a one-game ban, which we lost to the Soviet side.

We started the following season with a 0-0 draw at Old Trafford but only won two of our first ten league games. A 3-0 win over Newcastle in early November felt like it might turn our season around but what it appeared to do was alert Newcastle to how well Jim had done. They offered him the job as manager and within weeks he was there. He was replaced by Trevor Francis, who took the job as player-manager. Having been in this position at Fulham, I felt the responsibility to be a proper professional and help him out. Some players found it difficult, going from being a mate and going out with Trevor, to calling him boss and communicating with him as a manager, but I wanted to draw the line right away and call him boss.

I think Trevor found it difficult knowing the players too. There were a few occasions where he seemed to question their honesty with injuries. He was asking, 'Can't you have an injection? Can't you do this? Can't you do that?' It provoked a bit of a frustrated reaction, because Trevor didn't have the greatest track record with injuries himself, and ironically enough he then got injured and missed most of the rest of the season. Some players fell out with him. But he was learning on the job how to pick up the skill of man-managing. It's an often misunderstood part of management – sometimes a manager replaces one with a good reputation for doing things, and has a lot to live up to. Jim was one of the best man-managers. Trevor was still a player, and there was no handbook on how to handle relationships in that transition. My good friend and team-mate Dean Coney was one of the players who fell out with him. It just didn't work out, so Dean ended up going to Norwich City.

All things considered, we finished the season incredibly strongly, with nine wins from our last 12. In the penultimate home game we won against Manchester United in the last minute. Andy Gray scored from a free kick and it was bedlam. We went back to the dressing room, exhausted, and then Trevor comes in with bottles of champagne. I remember Peter Reid, Ray Wilkins, Kenny Sansom, Nigel Spackman, Alan McDonald, we were all sitting there and I'm sure we shared the same incredulous expression. As much as it was a good night for the club, it just seemed odd. Okay, sure, it was always going to be one of those games. A night game at QPR, Manchester United, the biggest game of the season, and it was just one of those special atmospheres at Loftus Road. We dug in and we won the game late on. Then your manager brings down champagne? If it had been a cup game, maybe I'd understand. But we had another game on the Saturday, and we were at home again!

Perhaps it was something to do with the fact that we'd faced United in a great FA Cup clash in January, just after Trevor had taken charge, and we were narrowly beaten after two replays. If we were going to celebrate anything, it was that even though we finished in ninth, we still finished above United. It's still a strange thing to write and think about now. I'd never in a million years have thought I'd play in a team that finished above United in the league. We would, again, the following season, but again that would mean regression for both of us, finishing in 11th and 13th, respectively.

5

The World Cup in Italy

I'VE BEEN asked so many questions in my life but the one that has never been asked, and I'm only thinking about now, is my first impression of Bobby Robson as a manager. My experience at club level had been with Malcolm Macdonald and Jim Smith (and of course 18 months or so with Trevor Francis). Bobby seemed like an angel in comparison. He was a softly spoken man; you never felt that he was your boss in that sense. You knew he was but you never felt as though he was trying to tell you that through anything he said or did. He was a very welcoming man and the only way I can say it, even though it may seem extreme, is that his whole manner was as though he was taking you in as his adopted son.

The England squad he had at the time was virtually like *his* football team. It was players who'd been with him quite a while. He didn't make too many changes squad-wise either. He had an 11, and he just liked to keep it very tight and get everyone around him who he knew he could believe in and trust. That's the way he kept it. He was very loyal, in the sense of once you're in and you're doing your job to the best of your ability, you knew you'd be getting a fair chance.

When I turned up, I was watching a lot of games to begin with. Or at least that's how it seemed. Looking back, it's not a *lot*, but it felt like that at the time. I had so many shirts with No.12 on the back, just sitting there not getting on. You get two shirts per game. One you put on as a sub, the other one you might swap. I always came back with both of them because sometimes I was sitting in the stands and sometimes I was on the bench and never got on. That's how it was with him.

Was I raging? Did I feel that I should be playing? I was comfortable just *being* there, because of him, because he still talked to you. He didn't just suddenly bring you in and ignore you, you weren't just a number, you were still involved. But the fact was, he just had, at that given time, more belief in the person in that position. I wasn't needed at that moment, but I had to be prepared.

Even when friendlies came around, he never made many changes. He was a proper manager, a manager sure of his decisions, and maybe that helped me deal with being on the sidelines a little bit more, that he didn't make the big changes. He wasn't a rash manager, so you knew that, in or out, you weren't going to be treated unfairly by him.

The expectations of the media were in a strange place with the national team. Everybody had expected big things after the 1986 World Cup. Because of what happened with Maradona, and everyone deeming Argentina as cheats, the credibility of the England team went up slightly – could they have won it without the handball? It seemed to create an inflated expectation that we'd win the 1988 European Championship, so we – the English media, I should say – sold ourselves down the river again. We put the players under pressure, put the manager under pressure, then said the manager didn't deliver. He was getting abuse going to the World Cup. Changes had to be made, a new generation had to come in.

I suppose I was part of that new generation. I'd enjoyed a great time at club level but I never had any expectations that I should be in the England team. Even when I was called up, I never once talked about it in the vein that I should be playing, because I was happy to be there. Where I started from to where I was at that given time was an absolute plus. In today's football, that doesn't really happen, does it? It doesn't happen. I think in recent generations I can think of Dele Alli and Jamie Vardy who came up through the leagues and then just got their chance.

There was some talent coming up with me, though. I think I made my debut for the U21s with Chris Waddle, and he'd been around the senior squad for a while but was now starting. I'd played against Paul Gascoigne quite early in his career. I think in my first season at Queens Park Rangers at Loftus Road, Gazza actually kicked me from behind when I was ushering the ball out for a goal kick, running towards the Newcastle fans. Typical Gazza, I think he got a bit emotional. Newcastle fans were egging him on and he took a big swipe at me. That was his hello to me. He came from nowhere and then the press were pushing for him to be king. He had life and energy and character – when you're looking for change, you want those qualities.

David Platt's emergence into the national set-up was more understated. I think most people expected that with concerns over Bryan Robson's injuries, Steve McMahon would be the understudy, but David played well for Villa and got a chance as we got closer to the World Cup in 1990.

My debut was against Albania, at Wembley, in a 5-0 win in April 1989. We were 4-0 up when I came on. We were in a very, very comfortable position and I must have had one of the easiest introductions to international football. And, incidentally, the first and last competitive minutes I played for England before the World Cup.

I was selected for the Rous Cup at the end of the season and my first start came against Chile. The week before that I'd been on an end-of-season tour with my mate Tommy South, the owner of Purfleet. They had a trip to Magaluf and I joined them for three or four days before flying back for England duty. I remember there was a bar called Mano's. Behind the bar they had what I can only describe as a fancy dress Queen's head. I decided in my infinite wisdom that it would be a good idea to get behind the bar, put on the Queen's head and serve people drinks. That's what I was doing the week before my full England debut. Not something I'd tell my mum about, considering how loyal she was to the monarchy.

Drinking in football was a popular topic of the time. A few months after this, Manchester United would make a statement out of selling Norman Whiteside and Paul McGrath in order to address the drinking culture at the club amid the idea that it had contributed to the club's underachievement. I was a drinker but not a heavy drinker. I'd go out with friends and have a lager shandy, just to be social, and at the time I wouldn't think there was anything wrong with that because you train every single day and you believe you're running things off. Now, of course, with hindsight, and now the horse has well and truly bolted, I can understand that it harms your recovery, impacts how you deal with injuries and makes everything much harder.

You got a good warm-up coming out of the old tunnel at Wembley, though. I'd made that walk a few times as a substitute, when you walk on to the pitch and then go on to the bench or the sides. Wembley was so distinctive with the twin towers and the long walk. There was a gradient on that walk, so that when you came out you could just see the tops of people's heads and then you'd hear the noise. First of all it would feel like you were hearing it from that far end first because the fans were seeing you. It was an incredible feeling, especially knowing they were cheering the team I was on. The biggest crowd I'd played in front of before playing for England was probably at Old Trafford so this was the first time a big crowd had been pro-me, so to speak. I wish I could go back in time and feel that again.

The walk was long. For a normal game you might come out with five minutes to go before kick-off. At Wembley, for an England 3pm kick-off, you'd have to start the walk at quarter to in order to fit in the national anthems. There's more time to think, more time to size up your opponent, and then you start overthinking. I remember looking at the boots of the Chile players. Were they looking at mine? When I was a kid I wore Woolworth Wints boots. They'd get bigger when they were wet, so when I did start to grow and my feet got a little bigger, I just had to wet the boots to stretch them out. No Wints on the Chile team.

They were a confident bunch. The atmosphere and setting seemed to boost them. It was an occasion, even though it was a friendly. I don't get that feeling at the new Wembley. In fact, I think more people think it's a pain in the arse to get to. I think at the new stadium the walk is so different, the dressing rooms could be anywhere, it feels almost ordinary, but it should feel special. There should be things that are extraordinary. The little bit of carpet or mat they put out because of the studs, and you had to be careful because it was slippy. Even the fact that you have to walk through the noise, win or lose. You might want nothing more than to get out of there. That was the risk of being there. To lose it would be a nightmare but you accepted that for the feeling of what it would be like to win.

Well, we drew against Chile. It was competitive but not eventful, with a record low attendance of just over 15,000 because of a Tube strike. It was memorable to me, at least, especially considering the events of the week building up to it.

I played in a draw against Denmark and then at the end of the year started in another Wembley occasion against Yugoslavia. That was one of those experiences where all I wanted to do when I heard the final whistle was get to that dressing room as quickly as possible, get everyone's head together and ask, 'How did we win that, by the way?' They were absolutely fantastic. Robbo did brilliantly – typical of him. That's what he was all about, scoring two goals to win the game for us against a sensational team. But that was an incredible experience playing against that team. They had even greater players to come into that team, and what was to come with the political unrest was a huge shame as far as I was concerned. That was a team that should have won a European Championship and maybe even a World Cup. They were that good.

The winning goal came from a cross from me (via a flick-on from Steve Bull) and a finish from Robbo. It was his last goal for England and took us to 21 matches unbeaten at Wembley, which was a record. It was one to be proud of, considering how competitive the friendlies were. Take the next one, for example, when we played Brazil in March 1990. Maybe it was having had a taste of it, or more likely the identity of the opponents, but that was one I wished I'd got on for. I was an unused sub. Bobby took it seriously and was justified in his selections as we won 1-0. These results were good for momentum going into the World Cup, and perhaps I could say that the Yugoslavia win was even tougher. Either way, I didn't feel too despondent, or that I'd gone backwards in the manager's thinking. It was just that Brazil is a unique experience. Everyone in football would like to play against them; they're the Harlem Globetrotters of football. Perhaps you might have likened them to Manchester United, in that they had a glorious history and a name that made you want to make sure you'd competed against them … clearly, it was rarer to get the opportunity to play against

Brazil, but I respected Bobby's decision because those were the demands of the international team at the time.

All of that positive momentum we'd built seemed to go by the wayside as we approached the World Cup. It had been announced that the FA wouldn't be renewing Bobby's contract, and there was speculation that he'd move to the Netherlands to coach. Typical of our media, they decided they wanted to label him a traitor. You can tell a club you're leaving a year in advance now and, bang, you're some kind of hero and they want to write a story about you every single day and give you a big farewell, but not Bobby Robson. They wanted to call him a traitor.

We then ruined that Wembley record when we lost in a warm-up game against Uruguay. And, having felt I'd done well enough to get into the squad, I was worried when I got sent off against Manchester City late in the season for kneeing Gary Megson in the head. I was desperate to make the cut but felt like things were going against me. I had a double hernia and had to then see a doctor in Harley Street and have a cortisone injection either side of my groin, both groins, just to get me through it more than anything, with the thought that I could be going to the World Cup as a sub. Then I broke my little toe. That's one you just have to battle through. But it seemed as though the red card would count against me. A few of the FA jackets didn't really want me to go, on account of the thought that they felt it was wrong that I could represent England when I was suspended in the domestic league. Don Howe, who was my club manager at the time, and Bobby Robson, appealed to say I should go – their pleas were heard, and I was included in the squad.

The first game against Republic of Ireland was a draw. There was a predictably bad reaction from the press. Bobby's reaction was to approach his key players and discuss what to do in the next group game against the Netherlands. It had been described as a squad revolt in the press but it wasn't anything of the sort; it was the manager approaching some of the key players and asking for their thoughts on changing the formation. It was crucial that we avoided defeat in that game if we wanted to qualify.

The Dutch liked to mix it up, mostly with Ronald Koeman. He stepped forward into midfield and he'd become like the pivot, he stepped in to become a central defensive midfielder. So that gave them an extra body in midfield. So what Sir Bobby Robson wanted was to nullify them in midfield, stop them getting good possession in midfield where they'd be able to keep possession and pass around us. It worked out well for me personally because I was brought in and asked to play at right wing-back. It was a transformational moment in my life.

We competed against them throughout that 90 minutes. We had two goals disallowed, one of them from me giving the ball to Gary Lineker, but they said that it was handball. We competed a lot better and drew 0-0. It put us in a good position for the last group game against Egypt. Maybe a draw would put us through but we wanted to win.

As I said earlier, Bobby wasn't one to make drastic changes, and it was even more rare to make a big call mid-tournament. The more the press went at him, the more stubborn he became in certain ways, and I think that's a manager's trait anyway.

They don't want to be seen as making changes off the back of someone in the media telling them they should be doing this and doing that. Gary Stevens had done well. That's the reason why Gary, up until that World Cup, was always his number-one guy in that position, but he made the decision to keep me in, which suggested that he was happy with what I'd done. He put me in against Egypt in a position where I hadn't played regularly in years, as a right-back, but he stuck with me, and with Mark Wright scoring a goal, we got the result that was needed. I can recall Peter Shilton making a really good save from point-blank range.

We were through to the knockouts, where we'd face Belgium. It was the first time I'd seen Enzo Scifo, this fucking good-looking bastard who had so much talent and knew it. It was the first time I really understood about arrogance in top-level players and what it can mean in different ways of presenting itself. Before, I understood arrogance in the way everybody does, but there was something about believing in yourself in the way he did, a level above confidence, where you have the ability to make the game go at your pace. Scifo hit the post – his other memorable contribution to this game was being fouled by Paul Gascoigne, who picked up a yellow card. Something Scifo and I apparently have in common is winding Gazza up to foul us.

That game went to extra time and then all the way to the dying seconds. I'd accepted penalties were coming. I was trying to get as far away from the pitch as possible. In that moment I remember us getting a free kick, and I could see Bobby

Robson on the touchline. Gazza got on the free kick and he took a couple of steps back. Every time he stepped back, I was looking across at Bobby Robson, and he was getting madder and madder, seemingly asking what Gazza was going to do. I reckon he thought that, because it was the last minute, he was going to have a shot, regardless of it being about 45 yards out. That's what he was thinking. I was thinking that as well. For me, I'd got myself in a position, I think my hands were on my knees, and I just knew then, as far as I was concerned, my body was going to go into rigor mortis. I just didn't want to move. I didn't want to move anywhere near anybody, in case they threw the question at me. *Do you want a penalty*? The last thing I wanted was someone to ask me that because it was the last thing I wanted to do. I was willing the rigor mortis to settle in.

Then Gazza kept his stride in a run-up, and he just clipped the ball, and it faded to the right. And David Platt did what he often did, and shaped his body to connect a perfect volley and send the ball into the net. Was that practised? No. Did Gazza see something, or did David Platt tell him something that he was going to try to do? It was straight down the middle. It was just the worst position in the world. The only time it's common to have a kick straight down the middle is when you're in rugby union or rugby league, when it could just go straight for the post. But Gazza did what he did, so did David Platt, and the rest is history.

We were through to play against Cameroon. Howard Wilkinson had been watching games for the FA and he told us that it was as good as a bye. I remember that, but I also remember that nobody really took him seriously. This was in the dressing room after the Belgium game.

We knew immediately that the Cameroon lads were so up for it. Before the game, they were in the tunnel, talking to us, already wanting to swap shirts. By the time we got to kick-off, though, they were singing their songs, and they were seriously up for that game. It was an incredible contest, of physicality and mind over matter. And maybe a lot of the players who were on that pitch were preoccupied by the fear that they were all going to get beaten by Cameroon and have to live with it for the rest of their lives, especially when we went 2-1 down in the 65th minute.

Physically, it was just an incredible game. I just remember going shoulder to shoulder. I saw myself as quite a physical player when I played. I *had* to be quite physical. But I went shoulder to shoulder with a Cameroon player, we hit each other and I can't remember anything about the footballing aftermath of that collision, but I do remember that for around three minutes after that I felt like I'd been hit by a pneumatic drill. My shoulder and arm were buzzing with the force he hit me with. I remember Dave Beasant telling me after the game that he could hear the noise of when we hit each other. In that couple of minutes, I honestly thought I was going to have to come off. You don't want to. You'll do anything you can to stay on. So I did, and thankfully it got a little better. It got better for us in the game too – Gary Lineker scored a penalty near the end to get to extra time. He scored another *in* extra time.

We were through to the semi-final for the first time since England had won the World Cup in 1966. There we'd play the other finalists from 1966, West Germany. I'd come into the tournament carrying a couple of injuries and we'd played two lots of extra time in the knockout stages but, really, the thought of fatigue or exhaustion didn't even cross my mind. You could call it the momentum of a positive run but I just don't think it was part of the football dictionary then. If it's not mentioned, it's not something you even think about.

The cortisone was wearing off and I knew that what I was doing wasn't going to have good long-term effects. There's a picture of me and Mark Wright, who'd picked up a big gash over his eye in the Egypt game, and I look at it now and see two men who are going through the wars a little bit. But you do, and that's the experience of playing in a major tournament for England. Or, at least, it was my experience of doing so.

I've replayed the events of the semi-final many times in the last 30 years or so. It was an event, a big event, a series of moments, a series of talking points. The game sparked to life when Germany scored on the hour. Andreas Brehme hit a free kick. It deflected off me into the net over Peter Shilton. It's absolutely amazing how many people have told me in the years since that I blocked it all wrong. Any bloke who runs out, you're going to get there, your arms will move because they naturally do, and you're going to go slightly side-on to protect your groin. That's instinct. I was right-footed, so it was natural that I'd go in on my right side. There was nothing else I could have done. I did my bit. I closed the ball down and I changed the movement of the ball. I changed the pace of the ball – it didn't move faster. I've said it before, but I rewatch it and can't help but conclude that a more agile goalkeeper might have done better. I can recall my instant reaction: we were competing – it hurt that we were behind in the semi-final. That emotion was quickly followed by something else. Something stronger. *Oh my God, I'm going to be the scapegoat.* It was in my head and it took me a good two or three minutes to get myself sorted out.

Really, it wasn't until I was involved in helping us get back into the game that I felt a bit better. I hit a ball into the box, and Gary Lineker did well to hold off a challenge and shoot in an equaliser. Gazza came across and grabbed hold of me. That made a big, big difference to me emotionally. I immediately felt the relief rush through me. The next thing that was in my mind was to not make another mistake.

I remember Thomas Hässler going off injured and the momentum we got from that. Recently – and I'm talking within the last few years – my wife had the idea to watch the 120 minutes of the game again. It was the first time I'd watched it all back. As I did, I realised for the first time just how well we'd played, and how close we'd come. We were the only team that actually could have come away from that tournament saying that we should have beaten Germany. From day one, when we watched them in Sardinia, the Germans were absolutely incredible. The way they just flowed with and without the ball. Matthäus was just fantastic. Yet, in that 120 minutes, especially after Hässler went off, we were lifted. We stepped forward from that. And if we'd won the game, I think everyone would have said that we deserved to win that game – 100 per cent. Prior to it, people were talking differently, and perhaps saying we were lucky to have got there.

Like I said, it was a game of moments. Aside from the way it ended, or maybe just as much, the game is remembered for Gazza's tears when he was booked and realised he'd miss the final if we got there. I've faced so many what ifs from supporters over the years, and one common one is what if we'd got to the final? We'd have beaten Argentina, they say. I always say we wouldn't have had Paul Gascoigne. That's the difference he made. The lad he fouled made a meal of it, and I'm not a fan of the tournament system for bookings, because I don't think it's fair that a player can miss a final for a booking picked up in a semi-final.

We played three knockout games that all went to extra time. All of them had their own drama. A penalty shoot-out takes five minutes. Whatever level of football, I've got respect for anybody who actually says they want to take a penalty. The moment you put your hand up and say you want it, if you go and miss it, I'm never, ever going to criticise anybody. I know that I wouldn't want to do it. But to go and do it, it takes incredible balls to go out there and do it at any level of football. It's all well and good talking about it being in front of 100,000 people or whatever it could be in a stadium. It could be in front of 5,000 people. There's still a lot of people because, whatever it is, it's not about the number of people, it's what's going on in your head. All the negative side. You've got to imagine that you've got to get rid of the negativity before you can go and be comfortable. And if you miss it and you put it in an area where you know that's what you've been practising and you know the keeper's judged it right, he's been correcting his faults, he's made a good save, that's all you can do, really. That's all you can do. That's all a manager and a team-mate would expect of you. Stuart Pearce saw his saved. Chris Waddle kicked his over the bar.

And that was how we were knocked out of the World Cup. This incredible tournament we'd had, over. There's that moment of sadness, and believe me it was felt, but the prevailing feeling to me was to think, *Wow, I've played in a World Cup semi-final.* My life had changed and I knew it would continue to. Of course, now, I reflect and think, what might it have been like if we *had* got to the final, or even won. But getting to the semi-final, the first in 24 years, even that was so different to what I'd known. So devastation in the moment might not have been the feeling I had. If I'd played just the one game against the Netherlands I think it would have been a massive achievement for me and for QPR. Less than four years earlier I'd been playing in the Third Division. We had one more game, though, the third and fourth place play-off, which we lost to Italy.

However, we returned to a heroes' welcome at Luton Airport. Some people want to say that was over the top, it was only a semi-final, and so on. I think we have to remember that World Cup, it just wasn't all about football. There was a lot more to it. There had been negative press about the supporters getting their tents smashed up every night. There was a huge political debate around English fans abroad, considering what had happened at Heysel – the UEFA ban had only just lifted. Hillsborough had happened a year earlier. There was so much negativity around football, especially English football. That tournament changed so much. The ordinary bloke, who maybe worked behind the counter in a bank, who wasn't a football fan, had suddenly started supporting England. And it just made such a difference to people's lives as it went on. Pubs started to get people coming in and wanting to watch the football. And I think that tournament started it. They saw an honest team go out and give everything. They saw emotion from that team, they saw what it meant to the players to be there.

As a national team, we never built on what happened from that moment, but I'm convinced that it started the change in attitude in the English game. Everything changed forever and it certainly made a big difference in my life. Coming back into Luton, it was a celebration. There had been a lot of exhaustion. I can remember Gazza and his girlfriend on the plane. He seemed to have no energy. She was asleep on his lap. But as we landed, and we saw all the people there, and heard the reception, that energy, that buzz was something else. If defeat can be glorious, there's a case to be made for that memorable semi-final.

We had the bus, Gazza with a fake belly, Terry Butcher on the top of the bus enjoying himself. The number of people there, it was absolutely ludicrous, and it was just incredible. We arrived at the Crest Hotel to meet family and friends and as I got in my car to attempt to drive home, we had people virtually circling the car, going past. Some people followed me from there. I was living in Wokingham then, in Berkshire. The cars continued to follow. I went on to the A43 and across towards Oxford and I was thinking to myself, *Do they live this way? Or are they following?*

I was living in a place called Woosehill and, as I turned into my little cul-de-sac, there was a great big banner across the road that said 'Welcome Home', and there were people having a party on the street. I think I had about an hour and a half, then I went inside and went to bed. I was exhausted. Drunk on emotion. It took a long, long time to get that feeling out of my system.

6
Moving North

I MENTIONED that there had been a change of club manager, so I suppose I'd better mention what happened there. Trevor Francis was immaculate. He just had this aura around him due to everything he'd accomplished and the way he presented himself. Some players just have that thing that makes them come across like a million dollars, and I suppose considering he was the first £1m football transfer, that's appropriate. We'd be travelling wearing our tracksuits and Trevor would still stand out. Our kit manager, Ron Berry, would get us a lot of M&S food for when we were travelling, but Trevor would have his own food prepared in Tupperware dishes. The first time I saw it I was gobsmacked. In different dishes he had smaller items. One with lettuce, one with olive oil, salt and pepper, one with different meats, one with bread. He'd put the oil in the bowl and dip the bread in. It was the first time I'd seen anything like it. He'd finish eating then start reading his pink Italian newspaper. And yes, at first, we had this thing about us where it would be like, *Who does this guy think he is?* It quickly changed into watching him and observing his conduct and wanting to replicate it in our own little way, feeling that it might improve our professionalism.

Trevor scored a fantastic hat-trick at Villa Park in September 1989; the third was a strike of beauty. It was a shame that football in England was at such a low ebb; the ground wasn't full, and the reputation of the domestic game was still recovering from the impact of Hillsborough, so not as many people saw it as he deserved.

I got on with him, and I socialised with him and his wife. And then he became player-manager, and straight away, remembering how it had been at Fulham, I stopped that immediately. I wanted to treat him differently because he was the manager now. He was the boss; though that phrase was something that had been reserved for Jim Smith. Trevor was Trevor. Difficult when you're now the manager and you're still playing too. Some of the other players at QPR still felt that he was a player and that they were owed something; if they weren't playing, they were a lot more forthright in letting it be known. I was disappointed by that. He was our mate and we should have helped him. We should at least have given him the respect of letting him know we respected him as our boss, and we'd have those conversations between us, to which the answer was that he was our team-mate and not our boss.

Trevor could never have gone to Vegas and earned a fortune on the card tables. He couldn't hide how he felt, so certain players saw it. It could become a little bit fractious around the club. I saw it with my friends. Dean Coney had come with me to Loftus Road and Trevor just didn't fancy him in the side. So Dean went to Norwich and for the first time since being 10 or 11 we weren't going to be together. I was devastated at the time. The first time I played against Dean, I was playing in the three at the back and I had to man-mark one of my great mates. He was taken off in the game. It was horrible in the lounge afterwards, seeing his mum and dad and all his brothers, who followed him everywhere. It was seriously, seriously difficult. So it was safe to say Dean wasn't a Trevor fan. We signed a player called Paul Wright to replace him. He'd scored lots of goals for Aberdeen and came to London with such confidence and self-belief but then Trevor barely played him either; every time he came on, he'd score goals, and he never lost that chirpiness, he refused to let it get him down. Mark Falco had a few issues with Trevor, too, and wasn't shy in letting it be known.

Man-management is a tough side of the job for anyone and one you're only likely to get right with time and experience. Did Alex Ferguson, when he was at St Mirren, make all the right choices with players and say all the right things? Of course he didn't. Trevor would probably have held his hands up and admitted he got it wrong on some occasions, but there was not a chance he could do it at the time. It wouldn't have done him any good to do that. But look, Trevor went to Sheffield Wednesday, and was an even player-manager there, and he had a fair bit of success. That's a very big club, and I'm sure those fans remember those days as the most recent good times. He'd learned from his mistakes, understandable mistakes, the first time around. I'm sure he'd have done it all differently if he'd had the opportunity.

Don Howe came in to replace him. Don was a serious football man. He was also a seriously funny man on the rare opportunity you could get him away from talking about the game; he had such a strong voice, and a range of hilarious stories, stories he'd find funny himself, and you couldn't help but join in. In contrast to Trevor, Don had pedigree as a manager, as well as having done it as a player. You may be familiar with the video of Tony Adams coaching, the one where he's remonstrating with his arms. That's exactly how Don would be on Friday mornings when we were working on our defending. He was precise. The one thing I will say is that Don might have been better than Tony on Strictly! The one thing Don would do is show by example. He'd show you exactly how you should close players down in the style he wanted to. He'd shuffle his feet and you'd watch, finding it humorous at first, but when you started training and applied the technique, you'd find it working. He was brilliant at doing things like that, things that seemed small but brought subtle improvements to the way we defended collectively.

One time in training there was David Bardsley, me, Alan McDonald and Kenny Sansom. Don brought in bits of rope, and we all had individual ropes that we were holding with the player next to us. Don would kick balls at us and we'd have to intercept it, holding our positions as a four by making sure we had our rope. At first we thought it was ridiculous, though we didn't say that to him. We did it again and again, over and over, and we'd be getting at each other because you were having to pull the rope because the player at the side wasn't moving quickly enough. You took it seriously because you knew that you had to get it right repetitively, and then on Saturdays, without the rope, our instincts took over.

Don Howe brought exceptional organisational skills. For somebody who was virtually running for his districts, someone who excelled at county cross-country running in distances of 1500 and 800 metres, I found that I hated doing that in training. Don had us doing it a lot, and one morning it was so intensive that I actually threw up. Don gave me the finger. 'You're the team captain! You shouldn't be like this.' It changed my attitude a little (only a little – you'll still find me at the back of most pre-season team running pictures). The point is that I was now learning where possible to make these improvements, and I can truthfully say that without Don I'm not sure I'd have made it to the World Cup, and not just because he advocated for me with the suspension I picked up before the tournament.

I came back from Italy looking for that kick on to the next level, but everything changed that pre-season when Bobby Gould arrived as Don's assistant. I think it's entirely probable that I changed that summer, because experiences like that do change people, but Bobby seemed to make it his duty to refer to me as a big time Charlie in front of my team-mates. 'He doesn't want to be around you now he's played in the World Cup,' stuff like that, and it just wasn't me.

All of a sudden we went from a team under Don where we were very organised and precise defensively to this abrasive new style led by Bobby. He'd been manager of Wimbledon when they won the FA Cup two years earlier against Liverpool, and their style of being uncompromising and physical had been influential in the league. Now he was here as a coach and training became about physical battles and bullying. Get confrontational. Okay, you have to adapt to different ideas to evolve, but this was a squad that had players like Ray Wilkins in midfield. We didn't play like that, and changing that about our game came at a detriment, in my opinion. Perhaps the idea was that instilling some of that Wimbledon-esque aggression would take us to a new level. Maybe I was more resistant to it because Bobby appeared to have taken a personal dislike to me. I felt like he was trying to create a barrier between me and my mates who I'd played with for a long time. Mates I respected, who I'd earned the respect of.

I started the season a bit late, on account of an operation I had over the summer on my hernia. The first game I played was at Old Trafford, four games in, a 3-1 loss. But the following week we played at home against Luton and I scored my only goal for the club. We were already winning 5-1 when I made a run from deep in the middle, played a one-two and then cushioned the ball before shooting across the goalkeeper. The technique of the goal wasn't too different to the solitary league goal I'd score for Manchester United 16 months later. It was, however, the sort of goal that I don't think I could have scored before. I didn't make that sort of move with the belief that I was going to score a goal – I did it because of the fact I now felt that responsibility, because I was seen as one of the main players in the team. When you spend so long playing with cultured midfielders like Peter Reid, Ray Wilkins and Nigel Spackman, and you're captain of players like that, you do feel an extra sense of responsibility to express yourself, to carry the game forward, to do something with confidence. And, pointedly, the sort of thing we'd do before Bobby, the sort of thing that we'd grown to do as a squad.

In November we played a Zenith Data Systems Cup game at Southampton and I did my cruciate in a collision with my own goalkeeper, Tony Roberts. I had a bit of pain in my shin on the drive home but in the morning I was in agony, shuffling when I was tyring to walk. Our physio sent me straight to Harley Street and I had an MRI, where I was told I'd damaged my cruciate ligament.

During my time out things went from bad to worse. On New Year's morning, 1991, I was driving up to Sheffield for our game at Bramall Lane and there was a brown Ford Granada right on my tail. I wondered what was happening, so I pulled over and so did they. And then the great big blue lights popped out. I was tested for drink driving. In fact, it was brand-new legislation at the time to breathalyse people the morning after. My last drink on New Year's Eve had been over ten hours earlier, but there was enough in my system to say I was over. I was taken to Chelmsford police station to do another test with the machine. One of the officers said they were going to get a doctor in to do a blood test, but it might take 20 minutes or so.

'While you're in here,' one officer says to me, 'go to the toilet and maybe go and get a sweat on.' But at the time, I was frustrated. I had my ego and I thought he was taking the piss out of me. I thought to myself, they've got a camera here, they want to see me go and do sit-ups to get some sweat going to get it out of my system. Now, I'd take their advice and maybe when the test came around I'd be under the limit. I was still over, and that found its way into the news. On my mum's birthday, 6 January, one newspaper had a picture of me with Jimmy Greaves and George Best, and the headline was something predictable about footballers who drink to excess. It was a stretch to include me alongside names like that, with a ball or with a bottle. The funny thing was that Danny Greaves, Jimmy's son, was one of my mates. I'd often be around Jimmy's house and he'd have beers in his fridge, and every time I was around he'd offer one.

Mum was disappointed enough with that. Dad went into a period of mourning, he was so disappointed with me. Don Howe was raging at me. I was banned from driving for 12 months and I hated having to rely on people. People have different tolerance levels to alcohol. I'd absolutely never drive when drunk, or even if I felt under the influence, and I felt fine when I did drive, but I did learn a lesson.

It was a difficult time in my life, particularly coming as it did straight after an incredible high. You have a hope and expectation for things to progress, but I'd been faced with a few different challenges. As the season drew to a close, and I was back in the side, we stabilised our form to finish in 12th position, thanks to the goals of Les Ferdinand and Roy Wegerle. Don Howe left; Bobby had gone well before him, to manage at West Brom. I couldn't say I was knocking the door down wanting to leave, but it definitely didn't feel like the same place it had once been. David Bulstrode, who'd brought me to the club, had sold QPR to Richard Thompson, whose family owned Windsor Racecourse.

Richard was a young man, and a lovely man, but he brought in Gerry Francis to succeed Don, and it was obvious right away that Gerry didn't like me. That might have been due to the fact that I was an asset to raise money for transfers, but it couldn't have been more evident that my time at the club was coming to an end. Gerry introduced a thing in pre-season training called 'Terror Tuesdays'. Running for the sake of running, from one edge of the box to the other edge with no end. Bleep tests without the bleep. You go until you give up. It wasn't my kind of running – give me A to B. Give me a purpose.

We went to Sweden for pre-season and I wasn't starting games. I came on in one, and it may sound far-fetched but I scored from about 30 yards. I went over the top with my celebration, the lads went mad, and for the first time in a while I was feeling good and thinking I was just going to enjoy the day and night. In fact, it was going to be a long one, because summer in Sweden meant daylight until midnight, and just as I was getting ready to go out, Gerry comes and knocks on my door.

'You're going back to London.'

I pulled a face but, smiling, I replied, 'What, because I scored?'

'No, you're going back to talk to Arsenal.'

'Well, I don't think I'm really interested. I want to stay. I want to go out and be with the lads.'

But Gerry insisted, and I was soon on a flight back to England. I should have been thinking, *Great, I'm about to go and sign for the new league champions.* At the time, though, Rangers were one of the best sides in London. Yeah, we weren't going to win the league, and maybe at that point weren't even in the fight for Europe, but I was very insular and, as far as I was concerned, this was my team and I was playing for one of the best sides in London; we were competitive and I loved the club.

I understood, though, that I had to go. I went to speak to George Graham about moving to Highbury and I was sold the story about *the* Arsenal. Everything was *the* Arsenal. And George, a lovely fella, was talking about where I'd be playing. I asked if I'd be playing regularly, considering they had Lee Dixon and Tony Adams, to name just two fantastic, international-class defenders. 'We'll do this and we'll do that and we'll fit you in,' George was saying without any great conviction. My response was that I already was a regular in the England squad and I was a regular starter with QPR. Now, I didn't have any right to demand a starting place in the champions' defence, but neither did George give me any strong belief that it would happen. When we got down to the details I was even less convinced.

'Do I get a sponsored car? I've got a car at QPR,' I asked.

'Well no, we don't do that at the Arsenal.'

I tried to explain that it wasn't technically the club, it was a sponsor, but he said they couldn't get involved in that. He'd already admitted they wouldn't pay me more than I was getting at Loftus Road. So there was that, no guarantee of a place in the team, and no sweetener.

'I need to think about it,' I said, though I'd just about made up my mind.

'You've got to the end of today, otherwise the deal's off.'

The deal was off, then.

Richard Thompson's family had some sort of relationship with Arsenal and it was hoped that I'd go there without any fuss. When that didn't materialise, it became known that Paul Parker was available for transfer, and offers were invited. That news made the press, and the first club linked was Everton. Those links appeared to be very strong, and my agent at the time had a good relationship with a few Everton players. It wasn't something pushed by my agent, just a link, a few conversations, and because Everton had been successful in the 80s (and there was no real indication of how tough things were to be for them in the following years) it was something I did give consideration to. Thankfully, it was a period of consideration that took in enough time for Everton fans to voice their own opinion on the matter. I went into Loftus Road and was told I had fan mail. That was a few letters from Everton fans, telling me reasons why they didn't want me to play for their club – or should I say reason, and that was chiefly to do with the colour of my skin. Look, that was only a few, but that was my first impression, and it wasn't a great one. My mind went to John Barnes and the difficulty he had to endure when he first went to Liverpool. If I hadn't received those letters, I'd have gone and spoken to Everton, but

I just didn't want to put myself in that position. It reinforced to me how lucky I was to have what I had, because never once did I hear anything racist from fans of QPR, and when black players came and played at Loftus Road, I never heard anything to make me think, *I'm playing here in front of hypocrites.*

It's funny how life turns out. The next thing that happened was that my childhood dream came true. Tottenham Hotspur, my childhood club, made an offer, and it was arranged for me to meet up with Terry Venables at the Royal Lancaster Hotel. For me, then, it was a foregone conclusion that I was going to sign for Spurs. Everything felt right. The money was better, but it was never about the money, it was just the fact it was Tottenham and I was just basically listening to what Terry was saying and he sold it to me quite early on. Terry had his own character, as well, of course. He'd been at QPR, and alongside Gordon Jago and Dave Sexton was considered one of their greatest managers. He'd been to Barcelona. Everything was agreed. The conversation moved to general things – he was asking where I'd played my football growing up, and it turned out we knew some of the same people in Dagenham. It was the sort of wind-down you have before saying goodbye and agreeing to meet up and do the paperwork and finalise it all.

Then my agent's phone rang. It was Maurice Watkins, a solicitor acting for Manchester United. They'd made an offer and QPR had accepted it. I didn't know what to do. I hadn't been in that situation before.

Terry made it easy. 'Well you've got to go and speak to them, you can't be rude, you've got to be respectful, they've made the effort to contact you. You have to go and speak to them.'

I wouldn't have had the balls to say I wanted to speak to them. I don't know if that would really be something I'd do. And, truth be told, in the moment I was a little bit frustrated and even heartbroken, because the London side of me was thinking if I had an opportunity to play for Spurs, I'd stay in London. I'd just got involved with a wine bar with my mate in Brentwood, and the whole thing was just all coming together, but when Terry said that, I thought I should take his advice.

So it was agreed I would, but he said goodbye with words I'll never forget. 'You do know that once you get there, you won't come back.' Just so I'm clear on this and there's no confusion, this wasn't an ultimatum. He wasn't trying to suggest to me that I shouldn't go, that I should sign now, there was no putting pressure on me like with George Graham's 'sign now or the deal's off'.

Terry knew. To be fair to him, it might have been completely different if Maurice or anyone from United had come down to London and met me in a hotel, but to go and meet people at Old Trafford and to see it without thousands of people around it, driving in on the coach as a visiting player was completely eye-opening. The club almost sold itself before I walked in. I was still banned from driving at the time, so I was sitting in the car on the way up, thinking of the 200 miles it was taking and thinking it would be a nightmare. I considered it a negative. I was asking myself why I'd want to go up north. This journey is going to be terrible. But then we turned off Chester Road down to the stadium, and I saw all the cars parked outside, and for a second I thought we'd got it wrong, and that we were there for a game.

I went into a big room with a big table and it felt like a job interview. Maurice Watkins, Alex Ferguson and Martin Edwards were there. I was mesmerised by what was around me. I was looking out the window, seeing the ground, seeing the pitch, seeing all the empty seats. I'd never seen it like that before. Even when you went out for a warm-up there was always a lot of people around so you never saw that many empty seats, or empty areas, I should say, at that given time.

The one thing I can remember is that the boss suggested we just go for a walk around. He'd just take me and walk around the pitch, and I think that made my life a little bit easier, because I just felt a little bit uncomfortable in that surrounding. I was like a fish out of water; everyone knew Martin Edwards and how long the Edwards name had been associated with the running of Manchester United. Alex Ferguson, meanwhile, had come through a tough start at the club and had just won the European Cup Winners' Cup, so there was no questioning his credentials as a manager. He'd grown into his skin as United manager.

So the boss took me around the ground. We walked around the side of the pitch, and he was telling me where all the families of the players sat, where the old players sat, where the directors' boxes were. I said to him that I'd thought there was a game on because of the number of cars outside. He laughed and said no, that's just visitors coming to the museum. Museum? At

Fulham and QPR there was scarcely enough room for dressing rooms, let alone a museum. Even when he said museum, I remember clearly that my interpretation of what he'd said was that it would probably be a small room, similar in scale to what I'd maybe expect Fulham or QPR to have at the time. I didn't understand or appreciate that by museum he meant an actual museum, that the description of it would be just as one would associate with a museum about anything that wasn't to do with football. As we made our way to the corner of the North Stand and what was the old Scoreboard end, I went to sort of cut across the corner of the pitch.

'Where are you going?' the boss asked. Impulsively, instinctively, I retreated from the turf, and back down the dip. I can tell you now that I felt that was a fatal error. I didn't say anything. You know when someone says something gently enough to let you know you've done something you shouldn't have done – and he said it with a smile on his face – and they look at you as if you should have known, but you never did? Well, I walked around the back of the goal and I can remember the fear in my mind. I was shitting myself. I thought I'd fucked it. Overthought it, to the point where I was thinking, *Does he take me as someone who will literally cut corners?*

As we walked down the side of the South Stand there was this noise, the movement of feet, of bodies, people making their way into the stand as part of what I started to realise was the stadium tour. A full section of the stand taken up, a number that would be a considerable percentage of the attendance for a game at one of my old clubs. It was madness, like everyone had rushed through in a surge. And I felt their eyes as they took their seats; they'd have seen the boss, and would have thought, *Who the hell is that with Alex Ferguson?*

'What's that about?' I asked quietly. 'Who are they?'

'Oh, they've just been to the museum.'

In my naivety I asked if something was going to go on on the pitch. He said, 'No, they're just going to sit and watch the grass grow for a bit.' And like he said, these people just sat down, there was nothing else going on, they sat to watch the grass grow. I was absolutely and sincerely amazed. There could have been no other place in the country that could do something like that – maybe at Anfield – as at that time it just wasn't a thing. You wouldn't expect people to do a tour of an empty ground and just sit there.

As we got close to the halfway line, this one woman just shouts out, 'Are you going to sign, Paul?' Hell of a question. Even Alex Ferguson hadn't asked me that yet.

'Yes,' I shouted back. There was a cheer from the group. I'm still not convinced that many of them knew who I was.

The boss knew he'd got me. Maybe he thought he'd got a bit of a weak bastard as well, considering that we'd not even talked money. I knew that I had to sign, really. It wasn't about money. I had money and my dream already offered to me. This was different, though. You didn't see things like this. You didn't get to experience life like this. That day always sticks in my mind, and it's often something that will come to mind, even when I'm not asked about it or tasked with writing about it for things like this.

It would have been much easier to stay in London. Everything I'd wanted was there. Spurs were the United of London in some respects, a stadium I'd been to, a stadium I'd played at, which had seen some of the greats. They'd just won the FA Cup. They'd got the history of winning the double. Spurs vs Man Utd was the glamour game of English football, the two teams with the greatest tradition of playing great football. So what was it that caused me to say no to my club? I suppose it was the name. Manchester United. I'd grown up watching them in FA Cup finals. I'd grown up enjoying watching their star names play.

It didn't cross my mind that they hadn't won the league title for 24 years. I didn't think of the last couple of years of QPR finishing above United, about the manager being under pressure, and honestly, even their recent success in Europe and with the FA Cup never came to mind. It was literally Manchester United itself. I wish I could sit here and say I joined because of my burning ambition to win league titles and play in Europe, but it was just the name, the romance, the history. And even Terry Venables, at the back of my mind, telling me I wouldn't come back. Now I knew why.

I can't say that I've ever sat in the stands by myself and looked out at the pitch. It might be one for the future. But I've had enough experience of going there after I've left, of being on the other side, of seeing eyes on me when something isn't going right on the pitch. I was at Old Trafford for the visit of Fulham in early 2024. Fulham won it in traditional United style, scoring a winner in injury time, even though United had scored a late equaliser just before. It was my first time sitting in the Sir Alex Ferguson Stand, the old North Stand. The eyes turn on you. *What does Paul make of what he's just seen?* You have to keep your calm, even then, you can't show your emotion. That's not always easy when you care; and that will probably be no surprise to anyone reading this who's familiar with my views, as I'm often asked for them by the press. You always feel the sense of responsibility to the club. It never leaves you.

Of course, since I left there have been huge ups as well as downs, and in the first few years of MUTV being created, I did a lot of punditry work, and there was a fair bit of the green-eyed monster in me, because I was seeing such good things going on and you naturally want to be a part of it and you're just gutted that you're not. It hurts, in a way, because you want to be there getting that bit of glory because you've had it, the adulation that's going with it, the buzz when you walk off the pitch having won, the banter in the dressing room, the bit when you walk outside after being with your friends and family in the players' lounge. I'm reminiscing now, of times I haven't even got to in this book. Maybe I ought to go and sit in the stands and reflect.

Once I'd agreed to sign, that was it for me. I stayed up in Manchester and signed a couple of days later. Within 24 hours of signing, I was on a plane to Austria to meet up with my new colleagues for pre-season.

7
All Change for England

I'D BEEN involved in England squads for quite a while before I even got my first cap, but for a long while I was sitting in the stands, then I was sitting on the bench. When I was finally getting into the team, I was with a lot of experienced players: Chris Waddle, Peter Beardsley, Bryan Robson, Terry Butcher, Peter Shilton, Gary Lineker to name but a few. We made it all the way to the semi-finals of the World Cup.

Then Bobby Robson left and was replaced by Graham Taylor. Any new manager is going to have different ideas, but there was so much change in such a short space of time that it was difficult to come to terms with. Nobody is going to tell a new man, who wants to come in and do his own thing to make it his own thing, that it's not broken, so don't fix it. That's just human nature. It's also a part of football. There's always going to be change.

I wasn't helped by my injuries; I was included in Graham's first couple of squads but I missed a few games, and that's really when he started to make some big changes. Some players were left out, some decided to stop playing for England, and big focal points were lost. So was the team.

When I did move to United, Graham pulled me aside and said that, in his opinion, my game had changed. I was looking for too many short balls, playing balls into midfield, and he needed the balls to get forward a bit quicker. He saw Lee Dixon as the one who could play more of a style that he was looking for, and then he also gave chances to Gary Charles and Rob Jones, and I kind of fell away from the scene, as did quite a few other players.

In the summer of 1991 I was called up to the squad for a trip to New Zealand, Malaysia and Australia. I played in the first game against Australia and then we had two games against New Zealand, and the last game in Malaysia. I was just getting myself over my knee injury, and I'd played the back end of that season. Maybe I shouldn't have gone, maybe I should have rested, but you couldn't take any selection for the national team for granted, and felt I had to go and play.

Bobby Robson was so loyal with everyone involved, there were hardly any changes in the squad, let alone the XI. When I went on that trip, there were a lot of different faces I hadn't been used to. You begin reminiscing, but reminiscing in a negative way. I was looking around and I was looking at the players I was with then, and I looked at the players from the role I was with in 1990 and I was thinking to myself that this isn't anywhere near. There had been too much change, and too much of it unnecessary. There were no Robbo, no Terry Butcher, no personalities like Chris Waddle with his funny little quips; the squad missed those kind of characters, the ones to give that little bit of humour, the ones who had that bit of stability. It was just a complete change, one that didn't give me enough confidence and belief really. I felt I was there for the wrong reasons. I ought to say here that Graham was still unbeaten in the job. He'd have felt vindicated in those changes, so bringing me back felt like reintroducing some of the old guard, and I wasn't sure that it made sense.

I went there as a professional, and tried to tell myself that everything was fine, but the truth was I wasn't happy being there, and I spent most of the time on the phone to my agent trying to find excuses to get me back, even asking him on one occasion to just make up a porky and say a club had come in for me and I needed to come back ASAP.

I wasn't the greatest fan of Laurie McMenemy. He was just constantly so serious and I got the impression there was something about me he just didn't like. I don't know, and I wouldn't speculate, but it just didn't feel right. As a contrast, we then had Steve Harrison, who'd worked with Graham Taylor from his Watford days as one of his coaches, and there was a lot of silly toilet humour going on, which went beyond banter and just made it a trip that was thoroughly unenjoyable. I had to endure it right to the end until we played in Malaysia in the final game, even though I didn't play in that one. Gary Lineker scored a first-half hat-trick, and went on to add another as we won 4-2.

Early in the next season, Graham suffered his first defeat, at Wembley against Germany. I played centre-half. He just didn't see me, or fancy me, as a right-back. I wasn't a centre-half who was going to be launching balls everywhere, especially in a position that had become a little unfamiliar to me, so I was out for quite a while. I got into a few squads but I was travelling and not getting involved.

Results started to turn. I wasn't in the squad for the European Championships of 1992; that tournament went disastrously, with England unable to get out of the group stage. The qualification campaign for the next World Cup in USA in 1994 was just as miserable. By the time we played the Netherlands in Rotterdam, we went there really needing to win. Graham brought me back into the team, and actually said to me, 'If we get through this, I'm going to take you to America.' You get a phone call like that and you should be jumping around, right? Maybe if I was a newcomer to the squad I might have been, but I was unconvinced by it all. And were we really going to beat the Netherlands? Results had already been so dire that it was the last throw of the dice.

We were level at half-time and then there was the incident between Ronald Koeman and David Platt, where Koeman pulled back Platt just outside the box. It was a hugely controversial moment as the referee originally looked to have given a penalty. But I always wondered whether David had gone down a bit too early. What if he'd got into the box and then gone down – then there would have been no question. Penalty and, probably, a red card. Everyone was moaning about the decision to give a free kick and a yellow but he was outside the box. I just felt David could have taken that extra touch and made it impossible for the ref to avoid the penalty decision. Koeman stayed on and nothing came of the free kick.

Two big moments of irony followed within five minutes of that decision. The first was that a Koeman should definitely have been sent off. Erwin, Ronald's younger brother, made an attempt at removing my family jewels with his studs, but was allowed to stay on the field. A couple of minutes later, the Dutch were given a free kick right on the line of the penalty area. After a retake, the elder Koeman clipped in his shot over the wall to open the scoring. Soon after, Dennis Bergkamp made it two, and Graham's promise of my plane ticket to the World Cup depended on a distinct mathematical improbability occurring in our last group game.

We needed to win by eight clear goals against San Marino in Bologna – the same stadium where we'd played Belgium in the World Cup – before even thinking about other results helping us. I was with the squad but not in the team. Infamously, Stuart Pearce mistimed a back-pass within the opening seconds, and San Marino scored. My gut reaction was to turn around and look at the FA officials. Many of them were laughing. One, Glen Kirton, had his head almost in his hands, as he was devastated that had happened so quickly.

We came back, and won 7-1. It must be the only 7-1 in history that's gone down in infamy for the concession of the goal. England didn't qualify for the World Cup, and Graham's reign as manager was over. I remember a few of us having a few drinks that night; it was most definitely not a celebration, but it was also much more casual and social than I ever remember a national team get-together. And, of course, the mood was incredibly poor, the worst I can remember in my time with the national side. I remember reflecting to myself, thinking that it didn't need to be like this. And now, when I look back, I think exactly the same thing. Graham could have gone further. It shouldn't have felt like the end of something, when he should have been building on a great achievement. He just dismantled it very, very quickly.

He changed a lot of things. Little things, like he got us to bring our own cars to Burnham Beeches hotel, where we trained. The idea was that we'd be there together, in our bubble. He'd always tell you where you're going, what you're doing. I was living quite local in Wokingham, which was just up the road from Burnham Beeches.s. So sometimes I'd be able to go home, but he took that away and the FA started to spend fortunes driving everyone in cars to the hotel so they were stuck there, even those of us who could easily go home.

It got to be that, if you got called up for England, you didn't want to go; you didn't enjoy going. When you're sitting there in a dressing room at The Cliff and you had the likes of Sparky, or especially Clayton Blackmore, proud Welsh lads, or the Irish or Scottish boys, they couldn't wait to go and represent their countries. I'd go and see the change in the staff, the change in the mood, the change in the atmosphere, so much of it brought upon by unnecessary changes in a short space of time. When that happens at a football club, they usually get relegated.

I'd gone from being a newcomer to almost one of the old boys, as such. I think John Barnes was still in squads, and David Platt, who both had relationships with Graham Taylor before. So the messages from Graham would be like, 'Oh,

John, you know this,' or 'David, you know this.' It was always to them because they knew it. I understand that this all may come across as sour grapes, but I understand why I had to earn my place and fight to get back in, because I had a few injury problems when I came back after the World Cup. But I think anyone analysing what went wrong in that period would start with the number of changes. The changes made it very difficult and the people involved made it very uncomfortable to go in there and play.

I related to Terry Butcher and Bryan Robson, and there was Gary Lineker up front. Robbo had got to a point where he was putting his club before his country and he had every right to do it at that point, and even then he might have seen maybe Graham was going to look at something different. Terry Butcher had done his time and now had issues with his knees. And then you look at Gary. I don't know whether Gary's drive had gone, but you look at the way things were with him. Did Graham see Gary as somebody who was going to cause him problems? Either way, an example was made and his international career was ended.

I certainly didn't really enjoy it. I'd previously found it quite enjoyable just meeting up with players, all the coaching and everything was all so close, and it was like a little club, because they knew everyone, because Bobby Robson had kept the regularity of the same players coming in.

I have to give credit where credit is due, because I've been honest, but I still don't feel particularly comfortable talking about only the negative things surrounding someone who has passed, even if that was just my experience. I always respected Graham, and my respect and estimation increased even more when he talked about his time as an England manager and he called himself out. He questioned his own decisions, how he got things wrong and what he'd done. I listened to him a lot when he was doing punditry work on radio because I was doing a lot of driving then. He was articulate. His knowledge of the game and his timing of insight was always incredible. He never shied away from the mistakes. He always talked a lot about England. And I think that could be down to the fact that he knew he made mistakes there and maybe in personnel, decisions on the pitch, everything on that side of it. But then when you look at his career at Watford and Aston Villa, he was just so successful at both those clubs, and the indication of the respect he was held in at Vicarage Road and Villa Park could be seen in the fact he was invited back to manage them both a second time. I never played against a Graham Taylor team, and had an easy ride. It was never easy physically or tactically. It was always right. At that given time, there was no better person to get that England job than him. Things just don't work out as well as everyone hopes they will all the time.

8

Early Disappointment at United

I ARRIVED at Manchester United at a good time, and a strange time. My own career was obviously in the ascendancy. United's trajectory was. And the competition for places at the club had turned a corner. Denis Irwin had signed a year earlier, a full-back capable of playing both left or right side. Lee Martin had been the man to score the winner in the FA Cup Final to bring Alex Ferguson his first trophy as United manager. And that had inspired Clayton Blackmore to have his best-ever season for the club at left-back after Lee got injured. Gary Pallister and Steve Bruce were a solid partnership in the centre of defence. Despite the fact that it was inevitable I was going to take someone's place in that set-up, it was definitely easy to settle in. I can even say it now, I didn't feel any issues with anyone at Manchester United. It was very open, everybody was there for the right reasons and that was to achieve as much as we could. The European Cup Winners' Cup victory was a great moment for the club, something that when you speak to a lot of supporters of my age or slightly younger, some of them even think it was a bigger moment than winning the Champions League.

I did feel a little lonely, not left out, but as I said much earlier in the book, there was so much going on at the club regarding that night that being the new kid on the block meant I had to work to feel a part of it. I wasn't the only one – I joined at the same time as Peter Schmeichel, and Andrei Kanchelskis had only just signed too.

The two players whose position was first at risk from the arrival of Andrei and myself were Clayton and Mick Phelan. So those two weren't maybe getting as much football as they used to, but both of them were fine with us. It's not an easy thing to do, to be on the sidelines watching when you've been a part of it, especially when you've been involved in major parts of that club's history in that time. It's a very, very difficult thing to accept, and to really get yourself in the right frame of mind. I have to say, though, Blackie absolutely loves and adores Manchester United, without a shadow of a doubt, and everyone knows that. I think everyone knows Mickie's feelings about Manchester United, too. It's in his blood, Manchester United. Both of them idolise the club and it means so much to them, but when you're talking about Clayton Blackmore especially, you're talking red, white and black. It goes through his veins. He was a wonderful football player as well, and a very intelligent player. His strengths on the ball far outweighed what I could do in those kind of areas but I think maybe the boss was looking at the other side of it. When you throw a Ukrainian train in front of a full-back then you know then what's going to happen behind it. It's going to be a little bit more safe if the person behind is defensive-orientated and minded.

Not just that, but that was one option and combination in what was becoming a squad game. Substitutes' benches were bigger, there were more games and the manager had several different players to now execute different plans or to get through an injury crisis. The idea, or at least the way I saw it, was that you'd been brought to United to step in and get through it without the standard dropping. Obviously Clayton and I weren't like for like, but that was the point.

You might say that this point in history saw the squad game become a bit of a thing. Today, every team in the top two divisions has a squad. Some of the top teams have 30 players to pick from. A lot of managers have got too much choice and can't make their mind up because they want to appease people. There's certain players that they don't want to play because of the fact that they never wanted them at the club. The club director or sporting director, technical director or even the CEO has gone and brought that player in but without you wanting him as a manager. Squads are bigger than ever and yet one of the biggest talking points of the last couple of years has been around players playing too many games and being tired. We couldn't get enough of it, and in the early 90s we were playing more games, and those games were more intense, tackles flowed more freely, the ball was in play for longer.

I digress. I came to the club at the same time as Peter Schmeichel, so I can't speak of the difference he made to what went before, only of the difference compared to my previous experience, and the impression he made. He was certainly confident enough to say this is who he was from day one.

Pete knew his standing the moment he arrived. He knew his standing back in his home country, and the moment he started playing we knew how good he was. Previously, I'd played with Peter Shilton and I'd played with Dave Seaman. Dave was great, I played with him at QPR and at U21s as well. In fact, one of the reasons I felt more comfortable when I went to QPR was because I knew Dave from the U21s. Dave was a great goalkeeper but Peter Schmeichel was more than just a goalkeeper. Dave Seaman was decent with the ball at his feet to a point but he couldn't be an outfield player. Pete could.

You've got to remember that his stature grew as well when he was at United. There's a picture of me and him together on the pitch, but Pete's shoulders got even bigger and broader than that, and he was always trying to go beyond where he was. He wanted to always be better than he was. He wouldn't allow anybody to stand in the way of him getting better.

The funny thing about it is that he always thought he was better when he faced fewer shots because he hated people having shots. He wasn't a show-off goalkeeper. He hated people having shots from any distance. If someone had a shot from the halfway line, he'd run to the edge of his box and have a go at Ince or Robson for allowing that player to have a shot from there. That's what he was all about. Pete didn't want you putting the ball past him when he was warming up before games. He wanted you to put shots within arm's length so he could use his forearm and just knock it back to you, and he'd shout that famous shout that became part of the furniture at United. He gave you the ball to take a shot and he'd say, 'Go on, hit me wherever you want in my body.' It was absolutely amazing to see someone so brimming with confidence. *You're not going to affect me.* That's what Pete was like about everything. He just believed in himself. And why not? The boss had wanted him for a year, by all accounts. The goalkeeping position at United is one of the, if not the single most, high-profile positions in world football, and you might say the boss had added to that by his decision to drop Jim Leighton in the 1990 FA Cup Final replay. Schmeichel was the replacement a year on and it was a statement to say we'll go out and get the very best.

The very best, the elite, are unconventional. They have a different sort of mentality and they do things a little differently. The size of Schmeichel made the idea of going through one-on-one with him an intimidating one for anyone. It also gave him an advantage and a dimension that others couldn't have. He could use that frame to stop shots in a different way. He'd played handball in Denmark, and the way you use your body for that is useful if you're a goalkeeper, so he'd learned this unique way of saving shots that we'd see all the time in training, and it would come out occasionally in games. You'll probably be familiar with it even though it was almost 30 years ago – the star jump. The first time he did it in a game was, I think, at Goodison Park. It was an evening game, I remember that, and one of the Everton players went through. Pete spread himself and the ball bounced off his left arm like it had struck a post. He'd save the ball by any means necessary, using his feet before that became a common thing. Very good goalkeepers of the time and the elite goalkeepers of today are seen in that way because they have one thing they do a little differently. Pete did all of it, in one imposing person. He was able to move from a time before the back-pass rule came in, where he was already earning his reputation as one of the world's best, to adapt better than anyone and become the best without question. I've no qualms in saying he's the greatest in Premier League history.

They say goalkeepers have to be a little mad. One thing they have to have in their make-up is the ability to shrug off an error. Pete made errors, everyone does. But he'd never allow anything to affect his head. Watch any game back from the 90s – watch him after we concede. Every time he'll have had a go at someone else. I think it's human nature sometimes when you're in that position because goalkeepers, in a certain way, they're maybe the only individualists within a team. Even if he was at fault, the bark would be out. That was reassuring in a way. It was part of his routine that you knew it hadn't affected his confidence. Bang – he was back in the game. Being a great goalkeeper to the point where you develop a reputation for being intimidating means you've understood that mastering that position is an exercise in psychology.

Every goalkeeper looked to him and wanted to be doing the things he was doing. He was a rarity because he was a foreign goalkeeper in the top division and he was so distinctive. I'm sure he got goalkeeping coaches thinking about what they were doing, and maybe there were traits they thought that they could pick up, but there were things about Peter that were just impossible to replicate.

Peter was replacing Les Sealey, a tremendous character in his own right. Like Les, perhaps, Pete was so forthright that you'd get a bit pissed off, or he'd get on people's nerves, but he was so good that you accepted it was part of what made him who he was. If someone isn't doing their job properly, they've got no right to be shouting about anything. Pete had every right to be as he was and I wonder sometimes if he did what he did because he needed that to get himself right.

We quickly established a good rhythm and relationship in the back five but the most important part of that was with Steve Bruce, who was the key organiser in the backline. At United we weren't often under the cosh but it did happen. When Pete first arrived, opponents had the idea to put him under pressure, and in the first few weeks we played at Everton, Aston Villa and Wimbledon – teams who were keen to test his adaptation to the English game by sending in a lot of crosses. We quickly learned that he was someone we could rely on. The old saying in football is you have to win the battle to win the war – in some of those first games you had to accept that teams would come at you, desperate to earn the first corner, to do something to get their fans going. With Pete, we'd struck gold. When someone threw in any kind of cross, you could just hear that big voice bellowing as he came to collect the ball. I think it made teams think twice about how to approach it because he'd collect crosses with such authority and look to start attacks. He was brave enough to come and get everything. He fancied himself every time the ball came in the box. He always believed that he could catch them. That was applaudable bravery because you know that even then he was still having to learn how things were in English football, because when he was playing back at home in Denmark the goalkeeper gets a touch and it's a foul. He suddenly realised very, very early that it wasn't going to work that way for him in the UK. He understood the advantage of his frame. We did too.

My first experience of Old Trafford as a United player came in a pre-season testimonial for Sir Matt Busby against an Eire XI. That was something extraordinary in the sense of it being one of the reasons why I wanted to go to Manchester United in the first place – this reference to the history, the embracing of the club's tradition. When they do bring out the old, the old is sometimes bigger than the present. Before the game there was a match between the United and City old boys, featuring Sir Bobby Charlton, George Best and others. The fans seemed to enjoy that more than the game I played in. Nobody had reached the levels those players had and the fans were enjoying it. There was still a lot of nostalgia there, considering for years those United supporters hadn't really got what they wanted, which first and foremost was a league championship, in 24 years. Prior to kicking a competitive ball for the club, I'd received a timely message of the footsteps I was following. Even if we achieved that ambition, there was still the fact that those players had won the European Cup. We'd have to learn to walk before we could run.

Peter and I both made our competitive debuts a week later, in the first league game of the season at home to Notts County. I was in the middle, in Gary Pallister's place. I'd played at Old

Trafford before, but it was a different feeling going out and that being my home turf. I could sense there were different expectations of football from the second I walked out. Notts County were managed by Neil Warnock. His style of football was just the same to play against as it has been throughout his management career, and I don't think it's too unfair to describe that style as quite horrible to play against.

We won 2-0. Job done. Routine. But it took some getting used to. The size of the crowd was one thing but, as I say, I'd played at Old Trafford before. I think what shocked me was travelling away from home with United. All the home fans want to come out and hopefully watch their team beat Manchester United. I suddenly realised how big United's support was. If you got it right, you'd always feel like you were playing at home, as the away end would be so passionate and loud. There was none of this wait and see what will happen. They try to get behind the team straight away and I think sometimes it does mentally affect a lot of teams – more so when you get things right as well, and you start winning games. It was a completely different feeling of playing. I think it took a few weeks for me to really settle, really realise where I was. It felt like my whole job description in football had changed.

I felt so grateful in that moment. I was able to appreciate what we had and what we were able to play in front of. I think the reputation of United's away support being the best in the country is something that's well established now, and even when I'm working at a game where United are away, I'll get a few goosebumps from it. It's definitely something that other teams just don't bring when they travel. A lot of teams bring numbers, but they don't bring the same support as United do. It's not just about having numbers, the bodies there, it's about having a voice there as well. That's what they do. They make away games an occasion and that's why those tickets are so hard to get. Everyone wants to do it, wants to be around it. It's one of the best places to go to for some reason.

QPR have a loud following but they just don't have the numbers to go with it. That's the difference in clubs, really. Some clubs have got hardened fans. QPR have got hardened fans who travel away. They go up and down, but they don't get as much joy as Manchester United when they travel. Those people still travel, believing that they're going to enjoy their day.

The extra electricity that comes with United games is that every team seems to have their own invented vendetta, from their fans to the players. You suddenly saw players who reacted in a different way to when I played against them as a Queen's Park Rangers player. Players just lift their game to show their worth; maybe they wanted the opportunity to play for the club as well. When I first went to United, the club was still chasing what they deemed as the Holy Grail and people wanted to be around it. They wanted to be there, if and when it happened, knowing what a difference it would make as an individual and to be involved in something that was going to be so big.

I can speak in the way I saw it as a neutral before moving, and someone who supported a completely different club growing up. It didn't matter how many titles Liverpool had won and what they were doing, the way they were. Everything about United was that little bit more flamboyant; it felt a little more cinematic, magnetic. It was all there. There was something about it that drew people towards it and had them wanting to be involved in it, and, more importantly, as soon as you were through the door, wanting to win games and wanting to win trophies because it made such a difference. It grabbed headlines. It grabbed a following all over the world. And people had a go at that about United fans, that they had fans all over the place. Every club wants that because that means numbers. That means the club's doing well.

Look, I can't say that it was in my mind that I was joining United to go and win a league. I was joining what I deemed as the biggest club that was in my head, the club that I wanted to go and play for. So you go to see whether you can succeed but then the environment around the club was gearing around that league title chase and, because we were in the mix, I suddenly realised the importance of winning a league title, because I'd never been around it. And the talk from the outside shifted in tone; it was that United *should* have been winning league titles but hadn't been. There always seemed to be negativity about them in the press. No one believed in them. No one trusted them to go and succeed.

When you taste that, when you sense it and feel it, that change in how you're perceived from the outside, be it opponents, supporters or the press, then that does change you in a certain way. You look towards your people and even that changes, but you have to embrace it. In Manchester, football is everything. I was staying in the Midland Hotel, in the heart of the city, and football was all you saw and all people ever spoke about. As a player, that had to change me, in the way you have to take everything even more seriously. I was a driven individual, motivated to succeed, but you have to want more. It has to become everything, to the point where your personality changes, your game changes. Your ambitions change. I realised that's how it was for everyone, and you don't succeed otherwise.

I'm talking from top to bottom. On the staff were Brian Kidd and Nobby Stiles. They're just men you can have a chat with. Nobby was lovely, and you have your conversation and think afterwards, *Did I give him enough respect as a World Cup winner?* I started questioning things like that afterwards. How did he perceive me? I became conscious of everything, aware of how I was, worried because I just didn't want anyone thinking I was there for the wrong reasons. It was apparent that the boss had deep trust in the men around him, and he valued their opinion. Especially that of Brian and Nobby, legends of the club. Were we conducting ourselves in the manner that was expected of the men they played with?

Having said all that, these were feelings of those first few weeks and months, and you settle yourself a little. I knew the boss was renowned for trying to get men who were the right sort of character for the club, and I knew he was close to Jim Smith, so they must have discussed me. I don't think the boss made many mistakes in what happened in the dressing room, in terms of every decision, but especially the sort of character he brought in. I think every manager makes most of their mistakes through what happens on the field with players, if players can't fulfil the potential they have or fulfil the reason why they're there, because the one thing you don't know for sure is how the person is going to deal with the pressure on the pitch; you don't know the temperament of an individual and their capability to adapt, because it's such a culture shift.

I'm not going to come out and say I was absolutely perfect, that I got it, because I know I didn't. I know I didn't, initially. It took me a while to get into. I had a few frustrating injuries in that first bit, it didn't really help because I couldn't get a run going. Yet, even being injured and being around that treatment room, just listening to Jim McGregor – as you have to, because he never stopped talking – and others like him, you could feel the devotion they felt.

I was in the Midland for about six months. It was too long, I was lazy and I gave myself the excuse that I was settling in. I'd come up on my own and it just seemed easy for me just to stay there. I enjoyed living in the city. Everything was there on my doorstep, I got to know a lot of people around it, the staff in the hotel, people in the local shops. It helped me settle into Manchester but not necessarily into the club as a player, and I think the boss felt that as well. So I decided to get out, and moved to a place called Little Barrow in Rochdale.

Following on from winning the European Cup Winners' Cup, it did seem as though the signings of Peter, Andrei and myself were an obvious attempt at taking that extra step to win the league; the boss had been in charge when the clock ticked over 20 years without winning it, and he was determined to make sure it wouldn't go past the 25th. The approach to strengthening the defence seemed to work, as we kept 11 clean sheets in the first 14 games.

The 14th of those games was against Liverpool, a 0-0 draw at Old Trafford. I was injured but I was there and able to witness for myself the atmosphere in the biggest game in the country for the first time. In the week before it was just like everyone was revved up for it. The players, a lot of them were revved up for it. I'd never seen that. I'd been involved in derby games in London but didn't get revved up as big as anything like that for QPR or even for Fulham. Everyone was really switched on with an intensity that I could only compare with England's World Cup games. I saw a change in the way the fans were as well. You could just see that game was so important for that club not to lose. You just felt it deeply, even just being around it, you keep your fingers crossed and hope that everything turns out all right. It's a battle. England's two biggest clubs going at it when at least one is competing at the top; it's vicious.

Arsenal were another of England's biggest clubs and were the reigning champions. They were the next team to visit Old Trafford and it was their first trip since the infamous one where both clubs had been docked points for the misconduct of various players in a mass brawl. At Highbury in the return, Arsenal's win had sealed the title, so there was definitely a hangover of bad feeling going into the match. Not for me – I knew some of the players from my time in London. The two teams were competing against each other, which just shows how things were going in the right direction for Manchester

United, and for Arsenal at that given time. There was pressure on it and you could feel it. There was a lot riding on it because of our good form, and it was intense, but I could already sense it wasn't quite as intense as it had been against Liverpool or even Leeds. If I could say what the difference was I'd probably put it down to some individual hostilities between both sets of players. Again, I missed it with injury – again, we drew. Not the best results in those games, but not the worst.

I'd also personally been desperate to play in Europe, so I was disappointed to miss the first round of our campaign against Athinaikos. I was back for the next round, where we faced Atlético Madrid in the Vicente Calderón. My first experience of continental football at club level left such an impression that, whenever I work as a pundit for a European game, this one always jumps to mind. We were 1-0 down with five minutes to go – not a bad result to take back to Manchester. But then the great Paolo Futre scored a second for himself and his team, and Manolo got a third.

You can never take anything for granted because it can change so quickly in any European games. You can never pre-judge a team, especially when you're away from home, because there's always those kind of individuals who can make something happen. That moment, that lapse, that belief of being comfortable can quickly be wiped away in Europe. It still happens now with late goals, players falling asleep. It happened in that game in Madrid, in fact. Everything felt new to me. It was a major shock to the system how a game can change so quickly. It's one of those things where you watch for years, you see all the coverage going on prior to it and then you get involved and suddenly, when you do play in those kind of games, it doesn't seem like you've got to chase a goal. It's a different kind of mentality as a player and it's a different kind of mentality as a manager.

That result was too much for us to overcome back at Old Trafford, so that was us done in Europe for the season. I think when you look at Sir Alex, that was his warm-up period. I think after the Cup Winners' Cup, the whole thing about him even then, I'm sure, was that he was planning for serious assaults on the European Cup/Champions League, and every time he played in those competitions in Europe he knew what he needed to go further. We were hurt by the new UEFA rule restricting the number of foreigners you could play in your team in European competition. It wouldn't be the last time.

There was some European glory that season when we won the Super Cup against Red Star Belgrade. It was usually a two-legged tie but, because of unrest in Yugoslavia, it was determined over one match at Old Trafford. I was sad to miss out again – my biggest memory of that game wasn't that we won, it was the number of times I saw Steve Bruce get nutmegged. We were pleased to win but almost embarrassed to have done so; everyone was just raving about them and how good they were. Rightly so, obviously, as they were European champions. I'd played against Yugoslavia when I was in the England U21 side and we won; I did for the senior side, too, at Wembley, but on both occasions I came away telling everyone just how fantastic a team they were. Boban, Savićević, Pančev,

Jugović – just four of the world-class stars who could have walked into any team. If that country had stayed together, they'd have won a major tournament. Without doubt. After this, those players moved on. They were all over, playing for the top clubs because they were incredible. They were known as the 'gypsies' of Europe, but the way they played football and the players they had were absolutely incredible. When you see how well some of the countries have done since the dissolution, it's just sad to think of what that team of players might have accomplished. AC Milan took a couple of them, Boban and Savićević, and those two played a part in what was arguably the best Milan side in history.

Even though the celebrations for winning against Red Star may have been low-key and somewhat sheepish, it did wonders for our confidence. We won the next six games on the bounce, scoring more and more goals in the process. Ryan Giggs had started to make a name for himself on the left-hand side and suddenly, added to the team that had won in Europe, were two wingers who were electric quick, with and without the ball. By Christmas Day, we were top, level on points with Leeds, but with two games in hand. We'd both lost just once.

For me, a run like this was just something completely different. I wanted to play every single game. When you're playing for a club like Manchester United and you're winning games of football, tiredness doesn't exist. I wouldn't have accepted that, ever. You wouldn't want it, because your ego says you want to be there on that pitch when you win a game, to be able to walk off, to feel that satisfaction of winning and the adoration of the support. There's no better feeling as a footballer when that's going on. It had been a few months of strange experiences to get used to. One I was used to with England, but now more regularly with United, was walking out at Old Trafford with Bryan Robson leading us out. You never really felt that he was going to get beat, because you saw the way other people were looking at him and then you got that same picture in your own head. You could convince yourself that you're not going to get beat because there was always more concern about what he was going to do rather than what they were going to do.

Football doesn't work that way – you do lose. Football doesn't allow those things to be taken for granted, because whatever's on paper and everything about your facilities and what you've got and who you are, it doesn't guarantee you anything. You have to earn the right. Sometimes it doesn't go for you and it's a reality check. But then when it does go well, and you get a rhythm, all of a sudden there's an edge and there's a vibe, there's a feeling, there's an aura going around, and that's the position you put yourself in when you go to a top club.

For someone who wasn't used to that, again, it may seem like an odd thing to say, but you do definitely have to prepare to be successful. Failure becomes something difficult, even if it was something you were once used to. Failure at Fulham was relegation. Failure at United might have been losing one game of football, when people get in your face or destroy you in the press. That one game becomes the difference between going on and winning something. It's a different kind of pressure, and winning never lasts forever, so you need to be able to be ready to check your ego and ensure you're always doing the basics right just in case you get that reality check. I will say that, despite it changing so much, I loved it. When you do play for a top club, they're the things that you come up against.

We had two games in hand over Leeds, which was an advantage, but not a huge points advantage, despite how things might later be portrayed. We were drawn against Leeds in the FA Cup and League Cup, and also had to play them just before New Year at Elland Road, which meant three trips there in the space of a fortnight. The story was of Manchester United versus Leeds United but all the pressure, all the narrative, was on us. Could Manchester United win the league for the first time in 25 years?

We drew at Leeds in the league. So far so good. On New Year's Day, QPR came to Old Trafford and in the space of 90 minutes completely changed what the topic of conversation would be whenever I returned to Loftus Road. We were poor on the day. I think we played a new system and I certainly do remember that Andrei and Ryan didn't start. I think it was a 5pm kick-off and all of these things seemed to feel like a bit of a dysfunction from our routine. We were in the team hotel in the morning, we went to The Cliff and did some light training, and then did our matchday routine. You normally get a few hours to yourself and we never had that. Is that enough excuses? We were 2-0 down after five minutes. It was my worst nightmare. This can't happen – I left this lot five months ago. Everything seemed off, nothing we did went right and there was nothing we could do that ever suggested we'd get back.

We went on to lose 4-1. It was a historic day for QPR and they wiped the floor with us. They loved it, and rightly so. They were excellent. Dennis Bailey made a name for himself, scoring a hat-trick. That was his biggest moment in football. 'You shouldn't have left the Rangers', the supporters chanted.

The boss wasn't impressed by it. He hated losing to teams from London and it shouldn't have happened. It was his 50th birthday the day before. Not one he was likely to forget. The list of pre-match activities, it all happened, but still, at the end of the day, if you're going to be deemed a top side, a top club and top players, you have to deal with situations and handle it. You have to learn to handle change. We didn't. You have to learn from when things going wrong. The harshest way in life, and in football, is getting your bottom spanked, knowing why it happened and then it not happening again. You have to feel the pain sometimes to understand why you don't want that pain again. And that's why you have to look at it and say, when it comes to performances in certain games, in games where you should be winning – a lot of them when you're United – you do learn. You make sure those kind of things don't happen again on your watch. *4-1.* It's still the first thing most QPR fans say to me. Some things are more easily forgotten than others!

It was good for us that the next game was at Leeds in the League Cup. I already spoke about these visits to Elland Road and how unwelcoming their supporters were to me, but they turned out to be enjoyable trips to Yorkshire as far as results were concerned. These felt like important results where, in a battle against them, we'd proven ourselves to be the better side. And they were a good team.

They had a good young player who I was always up against, Gary Speed. Tony Dorigo, Gary McAllister, Rod Wallace too. They were decent, but when it came down to it, we were the better team in the head-to-head.

It's quite a vile atmosphere at Leeds. Leeds was different, something I never expected. Liverpool, you half-expect, but at Elland Road it's vile and it's bitterness and jealousy, to be frank. They have plenty of Yorkshire rivals but consume themselves with Manchester United. The atmosphere around those games would be different. We'd always warm up 30 minutes or so before kick-off, but Leeds went out earlier than that. We had no stragglers in our group at Leeds – you'd get ready and go out and back in together. We'd go out and we'd warm up for a little while and, all of a sudden, Leeds players would all suddenly run in and leave us on the pitch warming up on our own, and that's when it became eerie. Seriously, seriously eerie. In those winter games there was a mist in the air and made it even worse. There's whistling all the time and you don't really warm up properly. It didn't seem to harm us too much. We went a goal down but Clayton Blackmore scored one of the best goals of his career from a free kick to level, and then Kanchelskis and Giggs scored in the second half to put us through. More Welsh influence the following week – Mark Hughes scored the only goal to knock them out of the FA Cup, too.

In the moment, it was a massive run of results, a comprehensive point made that we could go to our closest rivals three times and not only not get beaten, but outplay them twice and knock them out of both cups. Clayton has since gone on record as saying that, with hindsight, he regrets scoring, considering what happened in the following months. I understand, but I don't regret him scoring. That put us through to the League Cup semi-final, and when we won the trophy later in the season it was my first-ever domestic medal.

Manchester United had never won a League Cup before so that was a little bit of history in itself as well. I don't want to come across that it's all about me but it was something big for me to do that. Did I think at that given time when we beat Nottingham Forest that we were going to lose the League? Did it cross my mind? Not at all, really, because I was thinking still about winning that league. It was still there to be won. It didn't suddenly disappear. There was a congestion caused by a backlog of games but I always say when I look at football today, if you're not having congestion in your season with games then you're not competing. If you are, well, you're on the verge of creating some history. You're on the verge of winning at least one trophy. So that means that you're having a great season.

I go back to my reflections on participating in the World Cup and feeling positive instead of negative at the end of that journey. It was starting to feel a little different at United. This was the most successful season I'd experienced, but the demands were still higher. We could definitely have a relaxed atmosphere around the club but the seriousness that enveloped the squad as matchday approached was something that took some getting used to. As you got closer and closer to kick-off, and you were in that last 45 minutes, there was a mood in the day. It would have been building from being in the Grill room and having something to eat together before a home game or in the hotel at an away game. You'd notice changes in attitudes in some players. Certain players would have their own way, some would become more focused, quiet, others might become more extrovert as was their nature. At the time you're not necessarily looking at it as a matter of survival of the fittest, because you know you've been selected to be a part of this squad because the manager trusts in your ability, but looking back now I can view the whole thing and understand that temperament, when it comes to representing Manchester United, is just part of the responsibility that you accept to absorb into your entire personality.

Too many good players have gone to United and failed, and people question them. They question their ability and they question their capability to settle. You don't want it hanging around your neck. In the 80s I remember Garry Birtles and Peter Davenport getting a hard time. Fast forward a decade or so and Juan Sebastián Verón was another famous example of a player who faced unjust criticism for failing to settle. Note that I said fail to settle, because that's a different thing to failing because you're not good enough, especially at United. The level of expectation is just extraordinary. I met Verón out in Brazil in 2014, he was staying in the same hotel as me for the World Cup, and what a man, by the way. He came across to me and he spoke to me. I was shocked, I was almost starstruck when he came across to me. Now that's something I do – if I see another footballer somewhere and I know them, but I don't know them personally, I still always go and say hello to them. Juan didn't have to do that. We had a brief chat about how many times I watched him play at Old Trafford. He was a fantastic footballer and I could name many more players who struggled with their time at the club for whatever reason.

There was one in our squad – Neil Webb. We all love those players who look elegant with the ball, someone who it seems like they've got enough time on the ball to put a three-piece suit on and put a lovely knot on a tie. That's what it's like with some players and that's what he was like. I'd known Neil quite a long while from his Reading days, and he was like a superstar there. I had a few of my team-mates at Fulham who are from Reading so I was around there quite a bit. Everyone knew Neil Webb, you just knew of his quality and everything about him. He went to Portsmouth and had a brilliant time there. He was always the focal point of everything in midfield, and his passing, his football brain and his confidence were absolutely incredible. I was with him when he first joined the England squad, and he was in a similar position to me in that he couldn't get a regular spot, maybe because of Robbo, but he was there when needed. Bobby Robson liked him. When he got his chance and then did his Achilles tendon against Sweden, it's just one of those things that happens, but the worst injuries generally always happen when you're in acres of space on your own. That's when you know it's serious, when something like that happens.

Prior to that, Neil was having a good time in a Manchester United shirt. A really good time. By the time I signed, Neil was coming back from injury, a year and half on. Physically he was fine but it's the mental side of it that can be tough, and Neil struggled with that, to get himself back to where he was. He seemed to have a conflict with the boss as well, and their relationship wasn't going right. Neil didn't hide it, and he wasn't doing himself any favours because, at the end of the day, there's one boss. He'd struggled with his return from injury and, as recently as the early 90s, an injury like that could change a career in a way it might not today. To go from everything seeming like it was perfect to fighting for your place at the club – I had a lot of sympathy for him.

It's easy to say that he should have sucked it up and got on with it. If you're talking about players having injuries and getting back from it and being in the right mindset and you look at Bryan Robson, you see that no one ever doubted him. Every time he'd come back on the pitch, and he never doubted himself. Bryan Robson was still Bryan Robson when he'd come back in the dressing room, injured or not. He'd be in there early and he'd leave later than everyone else. But that's Bryan Robson, and he was extraordinary. That's how he was and we're all different in our make-up, we can't all be the same. You don't criticise someone for not being extraordinary.

Having done so well up to that third game against Leeds, the rest of the season – barring the League Cup Final – was an anticlimax. We won just eight games from our last 24, and it derailed our campaign. It wasn't instantly obvious that this would be the case. For example, we were unbeaten in the first ten matches after the last one at Elland Road; however, eight of those were drawn. One of those was a 2-2 draw with Southampton in the FA Cup. It was a fourth-round replay and went all the way to penalties, which we lost. That replay and our progress to the League Cup Final meant that there were now a couple of extra league games to fit in and no obvious place for them to be played in the calendar. The boss appealed unsuccessfully to have the season extended. It meant that we'd play against Southampton, Luton, Nottingham Forest and West Ham in the space of six days.

We beat Southampton, but drew at Luton, where I came off injured, and lost the other two games. It meant we had to win at Liverpool to keep our hopes alive. I missed that game at Anfield with the injury I'd picked up, but my first impression of that ground as a United player was a sense of intimidation I didn't feel anywhere else. It wasn't quite as bitter as Elland Road but you could feel that the crowd were trying to win the game before a ball was kicked. The fact that a home win would stop us winning the league definitely added to that sense of occasion, and when we lost, it hurt, I have to admit.

It hurt more than I'd thought it would, if I'm being totally honest. I was a kid playing locally the last time I'd been involved in winning a league title. Even when things were going great at QPR and we were near the top of the table, never once did it cross my mind it was going to happen, that we'd win the title. I suppose I'd say I started to believe something was going to happen at United, and I didn't really know how to deal with it when we lost that game and lost the title. We finished the league campaign against Spurs, but it was the game a day later, Norman Whiteside's testimonial, where for some strange reason it hit me hardest. Norman was a legend of the club. There wasn't a great turnout. He'd left United a couple of years earlier but was still well loved and had been forced to retire early. I didn't appreciate just how loved he was until I went to the club and saw it for myself. I know for a fact that the low crowd for his testimonial was not a representation of how the fans felt about him; it was a reaction to the pain they were suffering after losing the title.

I can speak safely without ruining the story for you – everyone knows what we went on to achieve. But I sit here and reflect for the purpose of writing this, and despite the great things that were to come, it does still feel like a disappointment that we didn't win that last Football League championship. What I can say is that we learned from that disappointment, because when we hit a rough patch the following season, we were able to cope with it better. When the outside world was looking for a collapse, we pulled together and came through it.

I used 'collapse' to describe that reaction, because that's what most of the football public is familiar with. It's a term you know, even if it doesn't seem very fair. You'll know another word, closely related to it. Bottle. Did we collapse in 1992? Did we lose our bottle? There were reasons why we lost the league, certainly, and reasons for a difficult start to the following season, which I'll discuss in due course. But, as I was saying about Bryan Robson, people become very black and white about some terms in football, and usually adopt extremes to make a point. What happened was, although it's difficult to admit it, Leeds were the better team over the league season. I can talk about our confidence in the head-to-heads but the table didn't lie. You have to commend them – and the boss did. Over a proper Easter period of football, we lost our way in the race, and Leeds edged out in front. We could talk about the fixture pile-up. Many have. But we weren't looking around for excuses, and we weren't saying Leeds didn't deserve to win it. It was crushing for us, and we had to pick ourselves up. Easier said than done.

9

Changes, and a Certain Frenchman

OUR LAST game of the old Football League came against Tottenham at Old Trafford. It was the last game in front of the Stretford End before it was demolished and rebuilt in order to become all-seater. I'd enjoyed just about enough of the atmosphere generated by that famous crowd to know what I was missing when it was gone. When I first played there, there were still cages around the ground, and there was something intimidating as a visiting player about chasing a home winger towards that end of the ground. And, strangely, it was a feeling that was transformed as soon as you pulled on a United shirt; every person in there is encouraging you to make the tackle, or pull you towards goal, almost. When it was knocked down, it meant for a significant period of the following season that we were playing to a boarded-up wall due to the construction behind it, and that was strange. It took a while for us to get going in home games and I do put it down to that.

There were two significant changes in football over the summer: the creation of the Premier League and the abolition of the back-pass rule. I'll talk about the league itself, first, as

I used to pay it little significance, but as I dwell upon it now I understand the subtle changes that made a big difference to preparation for games. I've reflected before and just thought life went on, the game was still the game, and to a large extent that's true. I think I was blind to some of the changes because my move to Manchester United had changed so much for me. The Premier League brought a new level of exposure to English football. Like I've said, growing up, Liverpool would be the only team on television, and then there was the FA Cup Final. Television games had become more normal and, being at Manchester United, we had more than our fair share. For example, if I'd still been at QPR, and suddenly we were on television as often as Liverpool used to be, then I might have noticed the severity of the change, but because the move to United had already transformed my life beyond all recognition in terms of the spotlight, I can't say that the renaming and rebranding of the league brought any noticeable change in that regard.

But I look back and think about the practical side of it. Kick-off times started to change. We'd often play on Sundays. I can't say I was too fazed by that at the time, but now I can see that maybe my mentality was shaped a little by it. Saturdays at 3pm was the traditional kick-off but the Premier League seemed to place the game of the weekend on Sundays at 4pm. That was just awkward, more than anything. Okay, if you were playing Liverpool or Arsenal, it spoke for itself that it would be the biggest game, but if it was any other team in the league, it meant a more publicised build-up and then this team coming to Old Trafford would be up for it in a way that they might not be. I'm not going to say it was a leveller, because it wasn't, and results proved that we were strong enough to raise our game to deal with it – it's just an observation about the impact of increased coverage. They became more like cup ties, and the pursuit of avoiding defeat, getting a result, became important. Those games would become more physically demanding than they had been before, or that you might expect to get on a regular Saturday 3pm kick-off.

Conversely, I think it helped us in away games. We always had to set out to win games because the boss wouldn't have accepted it any other way. A so-called smaller team playing at home on television – they'd almost feel obligated to try to attack. Much of our preparation came on doing the work early, starting the game well enough to know we could control the match if we did. Opponents always knew what they'd get from us, and we'd never disappoint. There would be no dawdling – get the ball forward, explore all our attacking avenues, exploit the most profitable. Of course there's a lot of pride at stake all round, so playing that way, and winning, and being on television to be talked about, all of it's good for the confidence and momentum.

BSkyB had the majority of the broadcasting rights for the league and they were requesting more media appearances from players, so we'd be asked to do things. I wasn't a big fan of it, but luckily at United we had players like Lee Sharpe and Ryan Giggs (though the manager made a fuss of trying to protect Ryan from this sort of exposure), the young good-looking lads everyone wanted to speak to before coming on to the more experienced lads.

I look back and think of the adaptation in our schedule. We'd sometimes now have to train on Saturday mornings, and then you'd be sitting around while the other games are being played and the results come in. Saturday night, you can't go out and wind down, you have time you wouldn't normally have because you'd be travelling. But you still might be travelling, to an away game, preparing for the next day. It sounds daft, but the Sunday lunch is such a staple of British life, and Sunday and Monday games changed that for us. Today, schedules are repetitive – the days of the games change, but preparation now remains the same, so players aren't as affected as we were back in 1992.

But, as I say, I wasn't as affected as some others might be. United had already taught me that every game carried that cup final feeling for the opposition, and the coverage of the Premier League seemed to validate that. Certainly, ever since leaving Old Trafford, I've never known anything to contradict it, and each experience I have as a member of the press backs it up. Every single club in the league, no matter how much they might say otherwise, their biggest game is United. I'm writing this in 2024, comfortably a decade after the club last won the league. It doesn't matter where they are in the table. If I go to any club in London to cover a United game, I know I have to get there at least three hours before kick-off just so I can get a chair in the press room. That same team can be playing anybody else the following week and you can be guaranteed a seat whenever you walk in.

To finish talking about Sky's changes to the game, their *Monday Night Football* was Americanised with cheerleaders and girls with pom-poms. That was a difference, and it was quite entertaining even if it didn't last very long. Really, if you were a player preparing for a game, you didn't get to enjoy the spectacle, and if anything it became more about distractions that hadn't previously been there. Distractions, I mean, in terms of logistics. Football was on the clock. Everything was regimented. If the cheerleaders were out, they were in a certain area, they'd block off the centre-circle because they'd be doing something, they might have something going on pitch-side so you had to make sure you were warming up in a different area. The change was awkward. Look, we got used to it, and now it's part and parcel of what a player expects when they watch the game growing up and become a part of it. I suppose the big question was whether it was giving something to the game. Was it anything the game actually needed? You get used to it – but is it necessary?

The biggest change in the early 90s, when it came to how the game was actually played, was probably the modification of the back-pass rule. One of my strengths was my pace and, if you're not winning the ball from behind, I still always had that belief that I was going to get there first in the sense of to be able to get it off of their toes and roll it back to the keeper, or get there first and be able to make a tackle, rather than them getting a shot off or being able to play someone in on goal. So it was easier, in the sense that I could beat people to the ball and the first thing in my mind was to get it back to the goalkeeper, and he could gather it up. The rule change brought on a different learning experience, All of a sudden, I couldn't use the goalkeeper.

I was very fortunate in the way it worked out for me, that I played with two incredible goalkeepers predominantly in my career in Dave Seaman and Big Pete, and both of them were equally as good with their feet. Dave Seaman was a very good footballer. He was one of those goalkeepers that didn't go in the middle often when we were doing piggy in the middle or anything like that. Pete would want to control it and sometimes even be a trifle elaborate with the ball at his feet, because he believed in his own ability. That's what made him the force he was really, he had so much self-confidence. I was fortunate that I had the both of them, but the change did still make me open my game up. It wasn't the first change I'd had to adapt to. I'd played in different positions in a back four and a back five, I'd had to adapt to those changes internationally, I'd had to adapt to playing on plastic pitches, so, because I was so used to adapting, I think I coped with it quite well.

No matter how the changes impacted the game, superficial or regulatory, we had the best man in charge to make sure our focus was simply on winning games of football. The boss made sure our concentration was there in black and white and he worked tirelessly at keeping it that way. In fact, as we know, while he was doing that, he was learning how to use the new media face of football to an advantage.

I was a spectator for the first weeks of the new season. We didn't start well – famously losing our inaugural Premier

League match, conceding the first-ever goal in the rebranded top flight to Brian Deane of Sheffield United. We then lost 3-0 at home to Everton and I think the fact that it was the first game without a Stretford End played a huge role in the way that match went. The edge wasn't there, perhaps supporters were getting used to things themselves, and Everton had a strangely comfortable night, one they wouldn't repeat for as long as the boss was in charge.

If the supporters had a hangover from the previous season, I can say for sure the players didn't. There was just something missing, something not quite right, and at first I put it down to the redevelopment of the ground, but as the season went on, and I came back in to the team, it did start to feel as though something wasn't quite right. It's easy to say that with hindsight, because you could have asked me that at the time, and certainly you could have asked me at the end of the prior season, and I'd have said we had everything we needed.

My return came against Brighton in the League Cup then my first league game back was against Liverpool. We were 2-0 down but came back to draw 2-2. Clayton Blackmore set up one of Mark Hughes's goals with a clever pass, the sort of thing Clayton could do that few others could. He was unfortunate, Clayton, because he picked up a hernia injury, and the boss called me in to the team and moved Denis Irwin to left-back, and it was difficult then for Clayton to get his place back.

I still don't know a player who can strike a ball like Clayton Blackmore; he's got so much belief in his right foot when he's crossing and when he's passing, it's incredible, and it's a good sort of arrogance and confidence. You don't often say a player has a wand of a right foot, it's usually a saying for left-footers, but you could say that for Blackie; he wasn't exactly athletic or anything like that but his strength was how he could pass the ball over a distance. People rave now about Trent Alexander-Arnold but I'd argue that Clayton was an all-round better footballer. He could defend, he couldn't be bullied, and even now in the legends games he's exactly the same.

I've already said how well Clayton had done in 1991, and it should be added that, as a defence, he'd created a strong bond with Denis, Bruce and Pally. It was so well-bonded as a team and as a defence, particularly considering what they'd won. I must admit I initially felt self-conscious about taking his place in the team because he was an incredibly popular lad. I don't think Peter and Andrei cared too much because they were new, and they were foreign, so that helped me in a way, but it was definitely something I thought of. Never once did Clayton seem to have anything against me, never once was he anything other than a professional member of that squad who loved Manchester United as much as anybody could. I think it helped me that I was a completely different sort of player to Clayton, and Denis, for that matter. The manager believed in continuity, especially in defence, so I knew it was now a case of me playing to my best ability so that he could keep his faith in me.

I hadn't played as full-back at club level for almost seven years before United. The only proper time I'd had came in the World Cup, but I was reassured by the simple fact that the boss liked my defensive work. We had a defensive unit and, the way I looked at it, we had the five of us defending, including Peter, and the six players in front. The four of us playing in defence had to be able to deal with any one-on-one situation that came up against us on the counter, and our job from that point was to let the midfielders and attackers do what they did better than anyone.

After the Liverpool match, we failed to score in three consecutive games, drawing at Blackburn and then losing at home to Wimbledon and at Aston Villa. Villa and Norwich City had started the season really well, and United had a dodgy record against Wimbledon, so of course, after the way the previous season had ended, the vultures were circling around the manager. United are in crisis again. Like I said, something was missing, and I think if I was to describe it, without being too obvious about the player who came in, I felt we were perhaps a bit too predictable in what we were doing. I hate to say that, because we weren't so far away from winning the league the previous year that you could say we needed big changes. And I should stress here that in my praise for Leeds as worthy champions, I'm not attributing a certain Frenchman as the man who made the difference. I think that's unfair to Leeds. But I think maybe we'd become so reliant on the way Sparky brought everyone in to the game that it made our game contained in front of an opposition defence, and even though sometimes that was difficult for most teams to work against, some teams had learned how to cope, and we lacked that little bit of unpredictability that could make the most of our pace to stretch a defence. You will understand, though, how reluctant I am to use this as a criticism of the team I was playing in. Every single player was incredible. But it's only when you look at the extra ingredient a certain individual can bring, the magic only they can provide, that you can identify what was missing, because it's not there.

So, we signed Eric Cantona. And like I said, I honestly can't write here that I thought he'd been the difference for Leeds, because I'd be lying. I hadn't played in the game against Leeds earlier in the season, so it was more Bruce and Pally who had the knowledge of what it was like to play against him, and they seemed to love him. The story goes that the boss talked to both of them about him. If I'm honest enough to say he hadn't made much of an impression on me before he signed, I have to say how immediately that was transformed when he arrived. He trained with us. He was about 6ft 2in, carrying himself like he was 6ft 7in. We found out how much he'd cost. I was cynical. I saw how good he was close up. How could he cost only a million pounds? It didn't make any sense.

Later on I had conversations with Howard Wilkinson about it. He told me personally that Eric needed to be somewhere else; for a manager, with a player like that, to diagnose that and actually turn around and tell his bosses that he needed Eric to move on, that was a brave decision – or some people might say it's stupid. What's the point, though, in having someone in your squad when you don't think they fit what you want to do? Maybe that player is fighting against you every time you try to get him to do something, and you're thinking to yourself, he's going to affect the other apples in a barrel so I need to let him go. As far as I understand it, it was more a case of that, rather than Eric agitating to move, although there's the story that he ultimately requested a transfer, but I think the decision had been taken by then anyway.

Eric was very aloof. You find with plenty of players that they arrive and they're chatty … I'm not saying Eric wasn't sociable, but he was just off by himself, he was quiet, he didn't force anything. And we accepted it. It was fine. We went to Portugal to play a friendly game against Benfica. We were there to play a game, and there was no great tactical instruction about how to change to play with Eric, it was just natural. You could tell, though, from the first time he received a pass, from the way he controlled a ball in the heat of the action of a game, the way he was able to kill it and showcase his technical excellence, that we were talking about someone of a different level.

10
Training Days

EVERYBODY WANTS to know the key to success, and evidently Manchester United enjoyed so much success in the 1990s that anybody would be intrigued to know the secrets of Alex Ferguson's approach to training. I think it's important to look at the standards that were set earlier than that. I can't comment on how training was at the club prior to 1990, when the first trophy of his reign was won, but I can comment on how it was for the two years or so before we won our first league title. I can tell you that the standards that were set were the standards that were followed throughout; there was no wisdom of hindsight that I'm going to apply now. Everyone wants to know how he turned United into a winning machine. So this was my experience of it.

I wouldn't say the boss was an active coach or anything like that, in the traditional sense of what you expect from a coach. I think he knew exactly what he wanted from a session. He was looking at the session and he'd try to get that transmitted via Brian Kidd. If he knew that something was needed coming into the next game, if there was a picture in his mind where he saw something, he'd get Brian to set it up and work around that week or the given time. The boss would be around, just watching it tick over and looking at it happening.

Obviously, he'd have an opinion and come in if things weren't right. He'd come in and encourage all the bits that managers do. He managed and that's exactly what he was. The boss's strength was that he knew how to manage people, manage footballers, on and off the park, he just knew how to do it, to get the best from people and from training as well.

We all knew when we could have a laugh and we all knew when we had to be serious. There was no written rule. Having him around didn't mean that we couldn't enjoy training, because he'd be maybe the first one to crack a joke or take the piss out of somebody. But we knew when it was serious, especially when it was a day before a game or the lead-in to a European game or a game against City, Leeds or Liverpool. We knew then that he was going to be a tough person, because he was so focused on that and what he was looking for, to make sure that we didn't go out and get beaten.

The boss had this principle, and I always talk about this, because people get through games before they've got a big match coming up. They just get through it and say the win was the most important thing. As far as Sir Alex was concerned, going into your next game, you needed a good performance. So, if we had, say, Liverpool on a Saturday or Sunday and we had a midweek game on a Wednesday, a game that maybe we should have been winning and we did, but we didn't really play that well, that would bother him. He'd be worried about the mentality of individuals going into the game. He'd be worried about the rhythm of the team because they hadn't had a good performance, something to take in and be positive about. He knew that would transmit across, that maybe fans would feel the same and might become edgy – but if you had a good performance, everybody would be lifted. The fans would be prepared for it, knowing their team has played well before. And even then …

One time we beat Coventry by four goals at Highfield Road, but he wasn't happy. He thought we were taking the piss, that we were taking our foot off the gas. That's what he was about. There was no such thing with him as a win is a win. *A win's a win, it doesn't matter.* People use that as an excuse, so it doesn't matter. But it does. People are paying to be entertained. And the United supporters are paying to see you entertain and win games. You can't let your standard drop.

Sir Alex's view was always that if you're Manchester United you entertain, you're there to entertain. Yes, you win games, winning is important, but you entertain. You're playing for the biggest club. Big clubs entertain and win games well, because you've allegedly got the best players, you've got everything right for you to go and dominate and achieve, so do it in a fashion that befits the club.

Every time the standard fell below that, he'd let you know about it. You could never turn around and say, 'Well, boss, we won the league last season, not a problem, relax.' That would be like a red rag to a bull. It's gone. That's history. You're going to have to go and do it again. You'd never have found him talking about what he'd done. It was there for other people to talk about it and bring it to him in front of him if they want to talk about it, but he wouldn't start conversations by telling people what he'd won, because that was history.

Those standards would be obvious but would, depending on the occasion, stay behind closed doors. A case in point: if you played badly, he could lacerate you in the dressing room. Destroy you. Tear strips off the entire team. After giving us a dressing down, he'd go out to the press and he wouldn't throw any player under the bus. He'd talk about his team and say this or that wasn't good enough, but he wouldn't go out there and leave someone wide open to go and be a target as a consequence of something he'd said. It would be up to the journalist what they wanted to write about an individual, but they wouldn't be getting a head start from him to use him as part of their arsenal to have a go at an individual. It's not the way he worked. He didn't go that way.

After he left leave the dressing room, you'd be sitting there reeling, feeling you'd been hit quite a few times by Mike Tyson verbally. You'd go away thinking about it, but it's up to you then how you respond to it. Maybe 99 out of 100 of us who got the hairdryer, they thought about it and they came back and wanted to prove a point. They didn't sulk because, one, it was Manchester United, you wanted to be around it; and two, you wanted to make sure that you were playing regularly, getting the opportunity to get it right, and for him to come up and turn around and say to you, well done.

He wasn't a tactical planner. That's not to say he didn't plan tactics; he just didn't obsess about them. He had a folder that came out for big games, but he didn't have dossiers of notes, and I couldn't ever say that training sessions were tactical. He just believed he had the best players. You were given responsibilities and you were made aware of it.

As a defender, you had your own job to do. Marking didn't really change that much from game to game, really. You knew your position. You knew who you were going to be up against. If you didn't do your job straight away as an individual, you'd have to take responsibility for it. Jumping ahead of time to give one example – we had a game against Barcelona at Old Trafford in October 1994. Romário scored. I was meant to be marking him, but in the run of the game, Gary Pallister sort of took him off me. Then he went and scored. The boss gave me a bollocking because he said it was my man. As far as the boss was concerned, that was down to me, because he told me to do something. I wasn't going to turn around and start shouting at him, saying 'but Pally said this'. I just had to take it. It was my fault. And it gets mentioned. I think the boss has used that example before, that Parker should have been with Romário. He was right.

My excuse in the moment was that the dressing room had so many leaders willing to take responsibility and Pally was a big character. I trusted him. You've got to go with your team-mate. You've got to trust them. You've got to believe in them. There's a reason why they want to do it. It's the same as anybody who takes a penalty. You can't berate them if they say, 'I want to take it.' Romário was brilliant. He made a great run for the goal. We weren't the first defenders, or the last, he managed to evade. I should have done as I was instructed to do.

Sometimes it wouldn't be the specific player, but the opponent in general, one with a specific way of playing that would be different to what you might usually come up against. Wimbledon, for example, who'd come into the 90s still enjoying the fruits of that reputation they'd earned in the 80s, as I spoke about earlier. We wouldn't suddenly go out and get all the young players around and have them booting balls in the air so we could head them away. The boss always believed that when you've got the likes of Pally, and more so Brucey – because Brucey would go and attack everything anyway, just to compete with the likes of John Fashanu – then you had the tools already. We were quite physically strong as a side, very mentally strong as well, so those kind of things didn't bother the boss. He knew that we were always ready and up for that, even going through to midfield with the likes of Incey, Robbo, later Roy, and even Choccy (Brian McClair) to a point. When Choccy was playing in the midfield, he was just as tough or just as astute as anybody in that role. He did a great job in there. There were enough players in there to deal with most things domestically.

It's when we went into truly big games, the big games in the league or Champions League, when the boss would be looking for a little bit more. Those little extra bits, that's where he'd have a little bit more to say about certain individuals, about where they'd be. That was always slowly changing, because of the fact that Europe was getting on his mind. It was getting more into his head, because he saw United were winning leagues, and how European football was a different kind of problem to solve. So he was looking at maybe changing the style of play as well – or, should I say, evolving, adding. We were always going to be 4-4-2, but even then we changed, because when Eric came along it was effectively a 4-4-1-1. There weren't big changes in tactics or anything like that. Eric was the change himself, but there was no directive to say we needed to change.

Peter still did the same job. Defensively we did the same job. The midfield worked in tandem with Eric but it was never about having one holding player. It was always about having box-to-box players, high-energy players in midfield. They weren't going to turn around and moan or anything about it. Keane, Robbo and Incey were all box-to-box. They dominated defensively and they also wanted to make and score goals. If anyone tried to tell one of them that they had to sit and hold, they wouldn't do it. They just wouldn't do it. *On instruction*, that is. Their natural game just had it built in. It's just that when the team broke away with the pace they had, those players I just mentioned attacked to try to get on the end of the many chances. There was still enough about them as individuals and combinations to protect those areas where they'd been in; it would embarrass them to have to get back if there were holes. So it didn't happen.

Training in respect of the approach to fitness was also different to anything I'd ever known, particularly considering just before I'd joined the club I'd been subjected to Gerry Francis's never-ending bleep test. Brian Kidd used to take us jogging around Littleton Road, and we were never allowed to go past Brian. You could see certain players wanting to stretch their legs and get running, they wanted to run past him, but he wouldn't let you do it. He was always holding off. At Queen's Park Rangers, it had become a slog. Long runs. Hard work, hard work. You went to United, and it was quality stuff. Yes, working hard, but with a purpose. Working in bursts. Improving your acceleration. You get enough time to do the things that matter, and it was always more about quality than quantity. I think that's the way it was with the bigger clubs, the better clubs. Much more practice was done with the ball. If you're trying to keep the ball, you have to be just as fit or maybe fitter than when you haven't got the ball. That's the thing. It was quite physical, but it was physical with the ball. You were constantly made to ask questions, to make runs and change positions to keep the ball.

It's a hallmark of the best teams, and the best teams generally have the ball for longer periods, and work harder to keep it and recover it. Manchester City are, unfortunately, a good example in the modern age. They work so hard when they've got the ball. Players change positions. You have to be more unselfish when you've got the ball to create space for people. The style is different, but the principle was the same. That's what it was about. The boss wanted players to do that. Was he coached in that way? Was it as stringent as it is at Man City with Pep Guardiola? No, it wasn't. But as players we just kind of did it because we wanted that ball. We had an insatiable desire to have the ball. They all wanted the ball because they had enough belief in their ability and what they could do with it at that given time. It was so enjoyable. Kiddo would go down as the best coach that I had through my career.

One of the things that we became famed for during my time was our ability to score late goals. You may think that there was some trick to that, some work in training that came into it, such as the techniques boxers learn about endurance and counter-attacking. I can't ever recall any emphasis on economy of endurance, about soaking up in order to strike later on. When you look at fitness, you can take someone to run and you can get them to run 10,000 metres. They train for that. You see people who run marathons. People running marathons rarely train the 26.2 miles. You never go anywhere near it. So really it's about what's inside your head, what's inside your lungs, what's inside your heart if you want to do it. The difference was, I think, when you're at a football club – and most times it happens away from home rather than at home – if we were behind or anything happened in those last ten minutes, you could always feel a sense of energy from the support, but ultimately it's about the players; if, suddenly, they get that little bit extra – the extra called belief.

You could get two people and they could train the same. Roy Keane, for example. In fact, all our midfielders, Keane, Ince, Robson. Same training as everyone else does. You could monitor. You look at all their yardage, it's the same as anybody else. Midfield players generally are always deemed

Holding the ball in my school team picture

With my 1st South Hornchurch cubs team, my first team I played on Saturday mornings with

With Ian Hart, my oldest mate

Press shot for Fulham in 1982

Challenging Newcastle's Peter Beardsley for the ball in a 1984 game

Learning my trade at Fulham

About to start a big season for QPR in the summer of 1988

Proudly captaining QPR

Embracing Mark Wright after our tense win against Belgium in the World Cup

Living a dream alongside some England greats

The most agonising moment, as Brehme's free kick strikes me and flies towards goal

Fighting for the ball with Andreas Brehme in the semi-final of the 1990 World Cup

I was lucky enough to win several trophies with United but the Rumbelows Cup in 1992 was special, as it was my first ever winners' medal

A proud moment meeting Nelson Mandela in South Africa, although I didn't take it in as I should have

Celebrating with Roy Keane after one of us had scored a goal against Spurs. It was Roy this time – but it had happened to me before!

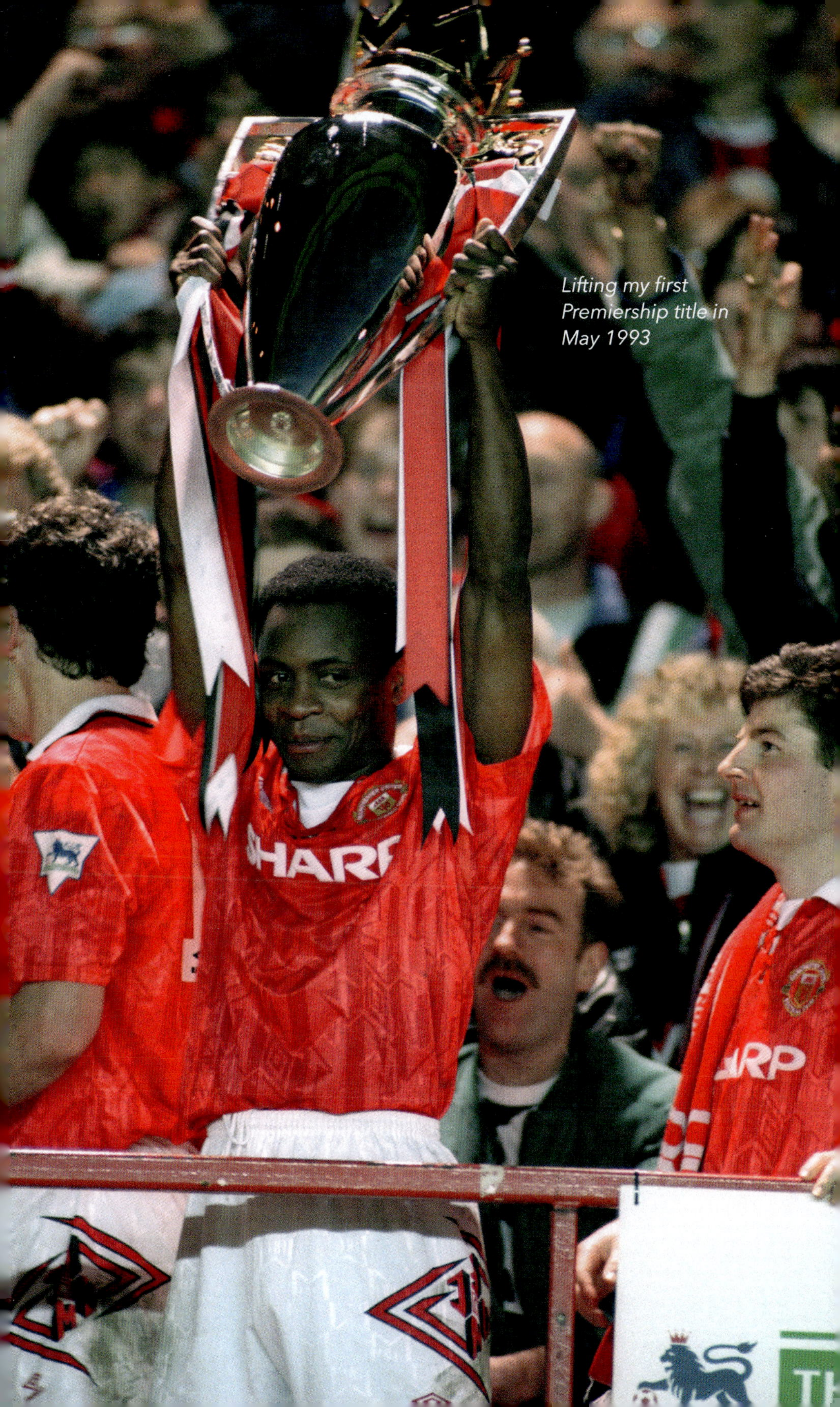

Lifting my first Premiership title in May 1993

A moment in history as we became the first Manchester United team to win the Double

With my wife Nicola

to be the fittest players, the ones who can put the yards in. Compare their numbers to most other people and you'll not see a dramatic difference. But in a scenario where it matters, there's a percentage that *does* make the difference. Somehow those three players would find another ten yards. They'd find another extra breath out of their lung capacity. That's coming from their head and heart and their desire to want to do it.

That's what it's about. It's about wanting to do it. When you want to do things, it's about you as an individual, but the other side of it as well, it's about respecting the people around you too. When you talk about Manchester United and you talk about Sir Alex Ferguson, it's that extra bit because the rewards at the end of it are greater than they are anywhere else if you succeed. It's something in-built in that sense. You'd bring someone, say, someone like me, and all of a sudden I've been at the receiving end of those last 10, 15 minutes and you're looking at it in the moment and you're going, wow, look at how Bryan Robson's running. And these lot, they're used to it.

Could he really train any harder than I train? Could he do more than I do in training? And the answer, when you're inside and seeing it first-hand, is no, because we only go to a certain point. But he found that bit when he was out on the park because everything around him tells him that he wants to and he needs to do it. That's what being at Manchester United does to you.

That was the mentality Sir Alex created at the club, but he didn't have to ask anybody to do it. He never questioned anybody while I was there about them not putting the yards in, them not running. You wouldn't do it, because, more than anything, everyone respected their team-mates too much. It's the worst thing in the world if your team-mates think you're shying away from working hard. It's the worst feeling in the world. I can't say I've really been around that too much, but you'd see it now and again. For example, if someone had to make a tackle they thought they normally shouldn't have had to make, if you'd stood back from it, they'd always let you know by their reaction after they made that tackle.

You could say that Brian Kidd's training with us, getting us to run at certain paces, tied into any thoughts about conservation of energy, but I just think it was a different energy when I was at United. Really, momentum is a universal thing in football, it doesn't matter what team you are – when you're on a good run, and you've got two or three wins behind you, it's amazing how the mentality of the players can completely change. They're willing to push harder, they've got more confidence on the ball because of that belief that everything's going well, the fans are behind them, they can't make a mistake, they're not going to lose. Everything is absolutely fine on that side of it, the individual. But what you find as well is the moment it does go wrong, players start to go missing at those clubs.

When you see the likes of – during my time – Sheffield Wednesday under Howard Wilkinson, even Leeds United under Howard Wilkinson, you look at Watford under Graham Taylor, Wimbledon under Dave Bassett and what they've done, and Wimbledon under every other manager, what they did. They were physical, and every time they trained it was about physicality. Bang, bang, bang. Those teams, when you look at it, forget about 90 minutes, you look at them over a season, and at the start of the season they're going away, they're getting shock results, they're getting shock performances. They were going to Old Trafford, they were going to Anfield, White Hart Lane, Goodison Park, Highbury, and they were causing problems, getting results, because they frightened everybody. No one enjoyed playing them, they couldn't deal with it. Players, in their minds, couldn't deal with it. Even though you'd prepared them, they couldn't deal with it, because the first ten minutes were imperative. Psychologically, even though the opposition individuals weren't anywhere near as good, they'd lost it. But those teams, at the back end of the season, a lot of them would fizzle away, because at the end of it the slogging is draining, and all of a sudden there were no rewards for it. All that slogging, there was nothing there. Obviously, they weren't going to win the league, the cup run had gone, so they lost that drive to go and push on that little bit more.

I used to see Wimbledon training when I was at Fulham in the early days. We used to train at the same place, a big open park, with just a pavilion there, a cafe there, and it was like Wimbledon's, it was like their training ground. They made a point of letting us know it was theirs. But when you saw the way they trained, everything was just bang, bang, physical, physical, run, run, run. And that's what it was all about. The moment you took that away from them, and that was by passing the ball, winning games, being comfortable, they lost it, that energy was gone. It was sapped away from them, so they just knew they couldn't compete anymore. So, the idea of it, when you're playing against those teams, when you get the ball, kill it. Kill the game, slow it down. Don't play at their tempo, because that means they'll cause you problems, because they want you to play in that tempo. Kill the game. Kill the atmosphere.

Mentality had been one of the biggest challenges for the boss when he arrived at Old Trafford, even if it didn't seem so by the time I'd arrived. Another of his inherited concerns was a drinking culture, which was around in football generally, but notably at United. I heard all the stories, and I turned up, and yes, the players did socially enjoy themselves. We did go out, but no one was excessive, and if someone was excessive, they did it at the right times and in the right places. We didn't live in a bubble. We went out all over Manchester. Cheshire, Prestbury, Hale Barns, Deansgate – we'd go out. We wouldn't hide and stay away from people. People were used to seeing United players out, and the same with City players. When I lived in Bramall, I used to go to a pub down the road on a Sunday after games, if we'd played on a Sunday. Of course, I didn't go when we lost certain games.

It wasn't like being in London, playing for QPR and losing the game. Where I lived, there wouldn't be any QPR fans, but London was completely different. You could hide, and you wouldn't get that many fans where I lived anyway. United, obviously, people would recognise you and they'd say hello, or they might even have something smart to say, and you'd just respond in the right manner. You'd end up getting them laughing because you talked back to them. It wasn't heavy. When you went out, you had a good time, but no one could ever question it because you were out publicly as such, and it was maybe three or four days before a game. Was the boss a fan of it? No, he wasn't. No one would be, but the boss knew that at the end of the day we weren't doing it two nights before a game or a day before a game. But everything in that sense was right. Socially, it was right. And it was an improvement from how it had been.

For me, I thoroughly enjoyed it … being able to socialise with team-mates, especially as a London player, as I've said on numerous occasions, you can't do so because you're living all over the place. Yes, at United we didn't all live in one area either, but we were all within a few miles of each other. It was easy just to leave a car and jump in a taxi. It was near on impossible doing that in London.

Times had changed but Bryan Robson was still the leader of the squad. On and off the pitch. You'd always look to him for a yes or a no for what we were doing. If Robbo said he thought we should maybe get out and have a night out or when training finishes, you'd go straight out and do it. You wouldn't go home to drop your car off and then come back. You'd want to be around it. You'd get FOMO (fear of missing out) if you weren't there. And it was everything, really – the buzz around the lads, the connection you'd make with the support.

Everything now with players is a little bit different, but the problem is that players are in bubbles and the reason why they're in bubbles isn't because they've made that the case, it's because society has put them in a bubble, has virtually made some of them into something they're not. They're paying the price for it by not being able to go out and maybe that has made their communication skills with the support quite poor. You listen to press conferences when players are talking. Doesn't matter what football jersey they're wearing, it's still the same thing, they're all the same. And most of the time it's totally uninteresting. You're not seeing anybody out there who's an individual, who thinks like one, and when you do get them, you end up with someone like Troy Deeney. Everything's controversial, everything's about himself. That's not a captain, that's just somebody trying to sort out his career after football. And lo and behold, that's exactly what he was like when he retired.

Manchester was good for me, it was enjoyable because I hadn't been around that kind of camaraderie. I love Queen's Park Rangers, I love what I had there, but it was a completely different kind of dressing room. And when I say dressing room, it was the training ground dressing room, not the matchday one, the training ground one is the one. Every player who retires is asked whether they miss playing. You get some who say yes, and you get someone like me going, no I don't, because I look at how big the pitches are, and I think, how the hell did I get around there? All over it. But I *do* miss that day-to-day bit. The close-to-the-bone stuff that would make you think to yourself, *Christ, that can't get out.* But that's the way it was, and there was always that trust and belief that no one was ever going to go and say anything, and there were many things said in the dressing room, many, many things said, but no one ever knew about it. It never came out, because no player would ever say anything to anybody, no player ever had the opportunity to tap on to their phone and to send it out there, send out pictures to go and do it, because Nokia and Motorola and NEC mobile phones never did that. It wouldn't be on your mind to do it, you wouldn't be bothered about having so many people following you, because you were more concerned about being around your mates, rather than worrying about so many people following you and thinking how good it is.

In theory, it was quite the opposite – you didn't want anyone around you, you wanted to be invisible, you wanted to go out, enjoy yourself without being concerned about who was watching you, or taking pictures. I've only had one pint, but they might come out and say I've had ten – all that. You didn't have to worry about it, and that's probably why players were more laid back and a lot more comfortable than they are now, and you see that in certain players' games, the way they play. The game now is very negative, and that's because life has made them that way, because of social media. They're worried about this or that, they're worried about their stats, because they know people look at stats. People don't look at, and judge, players on 90 minutes and what they do without the ball sometimes, but they keep passing and passing and passing, then all of a sudden it's a reference to a great player – he didn't give the ball away, out of 100 passes, he didn't give the ball away once. Then everyone starts going, *Wow, what a player*, so then you watch what he does and you suddenly find he's gone backwards and sidewards and everything is in the defensive third. I'm thankful that the environment we had when we were playing football wasn't overly obsessed with numbers. There was no false illusion about what defined greatness.

11

The First Title

ERIC GAVE us a new dimension. A release valve in the sense that most teams, or maybe all the teams, knew our strengths and tried to stop us. Eric came in and what that did first of all was to give them another body to concern themselves with. What Eric could do that was different was that he was always open, always available and always able to find someone else with the ball. We never had a player who could do that in that sense. Nobody did. So he allowed more players to join in than before, attacking in that final third. He added that extra bit of quality and that extra bit of improvisation.

When you see the modern-day so-called playmaker, they act like a playmaker and try to play the part, they try to overemphasise it. It's like they want a badge to show people what they are. Eric didn't do that. Didn't need to. He was just being himself, and it was his difference that set him apart. They call it scanning now – Eric knew what he wanted and he expected people to be where he wanted to put the ball. And if he did put a ball into an area and you knew you couldn't get there ... even if it crossed your mind, *Come on, Eric, that's a bit much*, you found that everyone would apologise because Eric has put a ball in an area and you suddenly think to yourself, *Yeah, maybe I should have been there.* It's either that or he was a really, really good card player, Eric. I think, probably, a bit of both.

Everyone talks about football. They analyse it. They give their opinions. Everyone said what Manchester United needed was a 30-goal-a-year striker. That's what we were missing. An Alan Shearer. A David Hirst. Today people still talk about what Shearer might have been able to do on the two occasions he didn't join United when he might have. But nobody was suggesting that United should go and get Cantona, or even a player like him.

We know from all that has been said that it wasn't a masterplan of the boss, either. It was opportunity and judgement. Eric wasn't a guarantee of goals in one player. But he was almost a guarantee of increased goal contributions everywhere else. Great sides become great sides because they have goalscoring threats in all different areas of the pitch. The most accomplished sides that have kept things going over a period of years, and have been the better teams over the years, have been the sides that have got goals coming from all different areas, from all different individuals as well, where they go and get their goals. That's what Eric did. He brought everyone else into the game and allowed players to gamble. Players would gamble off the back of giving him the ball and having the belief that, if you made a run, he'd find you. It wasn't long before we scored a goal that underlined that very point, when Eric set up the goal that Denis scored against Spurs in January 1993. The pass was sensational. The entire Spurs defence wiped out, not expecting Eric to chip the ball the way he did.

I'm talking about it now and trying to remember all the details that I became immune to because I was so accustomed to the brilliance Eric showed every time he had the ball. The game itself was fast. Our game was even faster. Eric had this ability to operate within that pace and yet make it move to his own speed. I can't say I took it for granted but you do just expect something different to happen. And, you know, when I look back now, there was a lot that *didn't* happen. But then, Eric kept having the ball regardless, and those gambles did pay off, and when they did it was usually spectacular. As long as Eric knew what he was doing was correct, that he was making the right decision, then he'd always keep trying to do that.

That's an attitude; it's not always to do with the spectacular moment or the level of skill. It's about not going missing. So if I say Choccy was similar to Eric with that mentality, you may raise an eyebrow, but Choccy was one of those who'd never go missing. If he felt he was making the right pass, he'd keep doing it and doing it. The difference between the two was that Choccy would always get a bollocking from the boss. Eric never did.

A couple of minutes after that Eric assist, Choccy scored from almost 30 yards. And a couple of minutes after that, I scored my first goal for the club. I don't know all the numbers but it was five minutes between Denis and me scoring. It's got to be the quickest in United history between two full-backs scoring in terms of time.

I played a one-two with Choccy. I question why he gave it back to me. I kept running in the same way Denis had. That was the usual way of Paul Parker doing it, after I've done my job, I've given it to someone. But I kept going, and I don't know why, really. I can't say I had the greatest intention of getting it back, but Choccy gave it back to me. I think it was Neil Ruddock who was sliding in on me. All I did really from that moment was just strike it, as I'd always been taught, to just go across the goal. It went in. The thing that blew it all was my celebration, because I had no expertise in how to celebrate. Literally, a handful of goals scored in my career. Sharpey and Giggsy came to me straight away. I was in shock, firstly that I'd had a shot at goal, and secondly, it's actually gone in. Textbook finish, as it goes. If I'm reminded about any goal, it's probably that one. It's probably the same with Denis and that assist from Eric.

We won 4-1. We'd scored five against Coventry and three at Sheffield Wednesday, when we'd been 3-0 down. The goals were coming, and especially if I was scoring, then you could say that there was a feeling that anyone could score at any given time. Most of the time I was at United, especially from that moment onwards, there *was* that belief.

I always say this, I'd come out of that tunnel, and I'd look around me, and I couldn't believe where I was and who I was playing with. It never left me. In fact, I'd say that the feeling probably grew. I never believed that we were ever going to lose games.

I go back to my back garden, in Rainham, playing football against my brothers. We'd pretend to be George Best, Bobby Charlton. As I've said, I was a Spurs fan, not a United fan, but I had an attachment to the romance of the club in the same way that some football fans just take a dislike through jealousy or whatever reason. The glamour was the FA Cup and United had been associated with Wembley days in my youth. Even their relegation and, dare I say it, even the violence that accompanied their time in the Second Division. There was an allure, an intoxication. Some form of glamour. They were the team that everybody talked about.

Then those vivid memories of my debut. Notts County. Getting cramp. A rarity for me, and it happened for no other reason than the sense of occasion. I was playing for Manchester United. Now I was scoring for Manchester United.

In contrast to the previous season, we were knocked out of both cup competitions early on. It's easy to say now that it helped us in comparison to how it had been an obstacle the previous season, but at the time there was absolutely no relief. The boss wanted to win everything. At the same time, you have to say that we benefitted from that freshness as opposed to being caught with a backlog of games.

Okay, so we weren't great in every single match. Nor was Eric. There's no point saying that, because the results prove otherwise, and we have to be realistic. The fact of the matter is, though, more often than not we were good, if not brilliant, and even if we weren't good, we now had tools to find a solution to get a result. Eric wasn't a one-man team. We'd come close enough to winning the league without him. The quality was there in all our other attacking areas. Maybe Eric coming in and doing as well as he did made other clubs lose sight of it. There were so many players with individual talent, it was incredible, and what set them apart was an attitude that said when it wasn't going right in their game, they said it isn't working out for me but the person I'm up against, it's not going to work for them either. They didn't just down tools. They had that inner strength to say I've got to stop my man. Sparky was one of them, Lee Sharpe, Brian McClair, Ryan, and obviously Robbo when he was still playing. They'd give nothing away.

This point can be proven in our return to Anfield after the trauma of the previous season. That's where we'd lost the title. This time we didn't have Eric in the team. I was used to going to Anfield and being treated nicely because we were just fodder at Fulham or QPR. It was eerie, the difference going there as a United player, as you'd expect.

The difference in our performance seemed to be control. No panic. We went in front. They drew level. It didn't take us long to score again. Sparky and Choccy getting our goals when it mattered. It was a relief to win but it wasn't the moment. We were still chasing that. So you win at Anfield and it's not the prize. Your eyes are still on that. You still have the focus. I knew how big it would be to win there but you don't really realise until you get back to Manchester, and those few days after, where everyone is on a high and the city was on a high. They told me Manchester was blue before I got there. That win was probably the moment I realised that was a myth. You couldn't move for people who wanted to tell you they were on a high.

The boss was an expert at reading body language. I used to think he was a mind reader. We lost at Oldham. Drew at home with Villa in a game we really could have done with winning, considering they'd emerged as our top contenders for the title. I think one of the biggest things he did to help us was to keep everything the same. There was never any panic. No need to make an issue out of anything. No player to be made an example of. Nobody who could be told that he couldn't be trusted. We were all focused on getting it right. We were learning. So was the boss. He'd made his warnings before. We'd suffered the consequences before. I'm speaking for myself here but I think one thing that helped us through that period, one thing that reassured us that nobody was going to melt, was what it was starting to mean to each other. I started to think that's how we all felt. That we'd take a rollicking from the boss, but our team-mates having a go, that would have been the biggest concern I could have.

People look at the Sheffield Wednesday game as a turning point. And it was, I won't say anything other than that. I do think, though, that people forget we played at Carrow Road the week before and put in one of our best performances. In its own way, considering the year we were about to experience, this was a catalyst too. I remember that we did something similar to Norwich a couple of years later, scoring goals in early blasts. Norwich were up there, challenging for the title. They badly needed to win that game. It wasn't quite as make or break for us but I think it was one of those games that someone could watch if they wanted to know what a typical Manchester United team under Sir Alex Ferguson looked like. We played emphasising all of our qualities, players making runs on and off the ball, players confident on the ball, a lot of pace, a lot of energy, a lot of imagination. Players working hard for each other. Players brave enough to go to an opponent in form and play their own brand of football.

Norwich were playing the sort of football that would be popular 30 years later. They were technically excellent. Ian Crook, Mark Bowen, Jeremy Goss, they had some fine players who liked to play with the ball. We were more aggressive from the off. I think the game was decided by a mixture of our desire and the sense of occasion. They'd played so well throughout the season but whenever the real intensity came they appeared to struggle. We were up for it. We were breaking through at will. It happened so often in the first 20 minutes. We scored three times – Ryan, Andrei and Eric. My memory of watching it all happen from my position at the back was that for each goal their defence raised their hands claiming offside. That was their reaction to it all. But we were too quick … we were just too quick. From the wingers all the way back to Peter, who could throw a football with the same velocity as a javelin thrower.

We reached an elite standard in the early parts of that game. People will remember years later against Roma when United hit four in the first half – this was similar. It was a standout performance. There was many a game I played in, in the back four, and just watched the front six. It was an incredible front six. Players get talked about now in terms of their position. A No.6, a No.8. Okay, in our time, we did have defensive midfielders, but to be just that in our team would have been restricting yourself. There was no room for it. You couldn't describe Paul Ince and Bryan Robson as defensive midfielders because they literally did everything you could ask for from a midfielder, whether it was a six or an eight or anything else. They had so much energy at both ends of the pitch and they dominated wherever they went. Robbo had been the master of that for a decade. Incey was never lacking in confidence but there's another sort of confidence that comes with maturation and he'd reached that in this season. There was so much energy in front of me, so much pace and intensity, that I felt as though I could take out a deckchair and just watch it with delight in the same way as the supporters were.

Of course there's a thrill, a satisfaction, associated with being on the pitch as part of a team that scores goals the way we were scoring them at Carrow Road. Nothing was over-complicated. It was the product of hard work and natural talent. It doesn't always work so well. You don't get those moments all the time. They don't arrive on tap – you don't usually find a performance like that in a cup final for example – but it's the pursuit of those moments of playing football and seeing it executed so beautifully that's as rewarding as anything. It just seemed simple – naturally gifted people playing football, people who were born to play football, no manufactured footballers. Everyone had their strength, and if their strength wasn't coming through, it was then a matter of, okay, we'll go out and we'll help someone else, and that's how it was. Everyone played a man and a half.

The match against Sheffield Wednesday came a few days later. This is a game I'm always asked about, as I'm sure is the case for all of us who were playing. People talk about the boss and his decision-making. I always say one of the best decisions he ever made was one of the greatest ever made to help a team win the league. People are lost when I say that, because you normally associate the substitute with the goal, and we all know that Steve Bruce played the full 90.

When Wednesday went a goal up through a penalty, I was the player brought off for Bryan Robson. Earlier on I spoke about my position as the player always first off whenever a team needed to change things up. Always the right-back. Always me. Enough for someone to get a complex, right? Sometimes you've got to understand the situation. My ego can take being replaced by Bryan Robson. I knew what the chances were of me scoring a goal versus Bryan scoring one. If he didn't score, then who better to come on than the man who'd inspired so many top performances in big games. The man who will either score the goal or make something happen. If I was thinking about my own pride at all, I was thinking about how desperately close we were getting to the championship and how much I wanted that medal. So no, I wasn't hurt, I wasn't spitting feathers, I wasn't calling the boss all the names under the sun. It was a manager taking a gamble, doing what he was paid to do, making a change to try to win a game of football.

That's why I have a moan today when I see reactions from players whenever they're substituted. There's always a bigger picture and the bigger picture is always the team and the result they're trying to accomplish. Any kind of physical and emotional demonstration puts you in a position of conflict with the manager, you're making it about yourself and not the team. If you have a problem with the manager, take it up with him on Monday morning.

A couple of weeks earlier we went 1-0 down to Southampton entering the last ten minutes. The boss didn't make any changes. Giggsy scored twice to turn it around. The context was different against Wednesday. The clock ticked on, later than either of Ryan's goals had been, and welcomed this period of time that has gone down in history. It felt surreal to be watching it.

Brucey scored the equaliser in the 87th minute. It was a great header, in the top corner. Everyone remembers it for Nigel Worthington being static, stood watching it, almost like he's glued to the post. My memory of that is something most people don't talk about. Robbo goes charging in, following the ball, to get it as soon as it's gone in. He's almost barged Nigel out of the way and, if you watch it back, Nigel seems so surprised by it that he almost stands aside, apologetic. Nowadays that would have caused a crowd scene. There's nothing aggressive in it, just Robbo following in, determined to either get the rebound or get the ball. It was a busy moment and everyone has their own memory of it. That's just my memory of it, something that rarely gets mentioned.

Home games *were* starting to feel like that Southampton one. We'd got through that, but since then we'd drawn at home to Villa and Arsenal. I know Pally has mentioned that the home game with Forest the previous season was on his mind. You do start to think about what's left on the fixture list. To have lost the game would have been awful. In the moment, to drop two points was bad enough, but you still have enough time to think that could be a positive boost heading into the final run of games. Who knows? We might have been here over 30 years later talking about the Steve Bruce equaliser against Sheffield Wednesday, saying that still helped us along.

There was also enough time for me to think about the fact that we were drawing, throwing away two valuable points, and I'd been a failure, because I'd been taken off. Take into account all of what I've said, understanding the need to help the team, understanding it because it's Robbo, but nobody likes to be taken off, and especially if it didn't go the way we all wanted it to. I was starting to feel as though I hadn't done enough.

It's funny to look back at a moment that was only half an hour or so of your entire life and consider everything you were feeling when you were just sitting, watching, out of control. Sometimes fate does come into it. Sometimes you're better just leaving it to fate. I say that in the position of someone who was on the bench, helpless to influence anything. Thankfully the others didn't leave it to fate, even if you might think fate played a part. You have to force the issue. You have to make your own luck. That's how you end up with one centre-back, Gary Pallister, crossing the ball for his pal, Steve Bruce, to run on to and score the winning goal.

And then obviously everybody's memories are the same. Brian Kidd loses his mind and runs on to the pitch. Alex Ferguson follows him but, perhaps seeing how Kiddo has jumped up and down, thinks better of the double knee replacement he might need if he jumps four feet in the air and lands on the pitch.

So we won the game. I'm thinking about Trevor Francis, the Sheffield Wednesday boss, my old manager. I remember how much he celebrated that meaningless win over United, how much it meant to him. Those were the sorts of efforts we'd had to put in to get over the finish line. Everybody doing their best in trying circumstances. You think of how much luck plays a part and you can give yourself a break from thinking, for a moment, that you'd failed. Of course, in that moment, there's only elation.

Who knows what might have happened without that second goal? Pally's probably right. Three games without a win at home, the media would have been all over it. It would become a complex. The manager might have been worried. Might have been tempted to make big changes. But even the boss, usually the calmest man in the room – when he wasn't angry – couldn't hide his elation after that game. He wasn't one to get carried away after a win, even in semi-finals, but this was one of those rare days where he couldn't stop himself. Nobody could blame him.

Back in training, it's all back to normal. Back down to earth. Nothing is won yet. We have momentum – keep it. It's one of the hardest things to generate in football. Wednesday were one of the better-performing teams of the season. They got to both domestic cup finals. They knew about dragging games to their death. To beat both them and Norwich, in the way we did, answered multiple questions about our character.

Bruce's winner became known as the first 'Fergie Time' goal. Observers and pundits were watching that game, keen to make some form of statement about our character, how we were going to lose the league again. But they saw growth, they saw a team determined to fight. Unwilling to accept defeat. And that became the thing that started to form in people's minds. We could play our natural game and beat anyone, and on the odd occasion we struggled, well, now teams knew that there would be no crisis of confidence. Just patience and composure, two qualities that, on a football field, can provoke the opposite reaction in an opponent. Teams wouldn't grow in confidence if they were holding us with 20, or 10 minutes to go. Instead, they'd grow edgy, fall into themselves, fearful of what might happen. It helped us have more possession and more time to find solutions. I'm certain it played a role in our conclusion to the season. I think it made teams confused from the off. There were three scenarios, all of which Eric came alive in. One, they'd come at us, and Eric could pick them off. Two, they'd sit back, and Eric had time to pick his moment. Three, even if they got to 80 minutes, Eric could sit on the periphery of a game, making opponents anxious because he was so unpredictable, enabling us to go about our business and trying to find a solution with or without him at the centre of it. It was a dramatic difference in comparison to the previous season.

We beat Coventry and Chelsea with some comfort before going down to Selhurst Park. Villa were playing at Blackburn. Rarely have I played in a game that had such anticipation around it. The main reason for that was the sheer number of United supporters who were at Palace. It was ridiculous. Mad. Getting off the coach, trying to get to the changing room. Honestly, the fever that had taken over was incredible. In football there's a saying: play the game, not the occasion. Sometimes the occasion is bigger, more surreal, unlike anything you could plan for. Liverpool went 30 years without winning the league and right when they were ready to end that wait the COVID-19 pandemic hit, the sport was put on hold, and when it came back there were no fans. In living memory there isn't another comparison, there's only this experience. Here we were, playing in a stadium that was renowned as being uncompromising. There were mostly United fans inside. At least three-quarters of the ground were United. The atmosphere was crazy – we were made aware that Blackburn were beating Villa.

You can't say you dream of a moment like that in football. You're on the verge of something historic. You can't contrive circumstances like the ones we were in. Manchester United had been 26 years without a league title – 25 had been tough, there was anxiety and hope and the excruciating taste of failure. This time, though, the odds were in our favour. If we could win this game, we'd only need to win one more from our last two, and for the first time in all those years the United supporters could finally believe it *was* going to happen. From my perception, it seemed as though the Palace players were a little stunned by it. Not by the idea that United coming to town was the biggest game of the season, but by what was happening on the terraces. It was electric.

At half-time it was 0-0. We found out for sure that Villa were being beaten heavily. The confidence we played with in the second half was fantastic – everyone stepped up a level. I think we had the belief that Sheffield Wednesday had been the big test, and we'd got over that. What was happening at Ewood Park strengthened that belief, and really that second half at Palace was more a matter of knowing, for the first time, that it was going to happen. Sparky and Incey got the goals. Eric was involved in both of them. Ince's goal was a minute from the end. The celebrations were chaotic.

The following weekend we were due to play Blackburn at home on the Monday. Villa had Oldham at home on the Sunday. If they didn't win, we'd be champions. Everyone at the club started off saying they weren't going to watch it. Insisting they weren't going to. I wasn't sure, really. I was waiting for everyone else. So when Brucey phoned and asked me to go round, that's what I did, and so did Incey, and big Pete, who both lived in the same area. Oldham scored in the first half. I think word was getting around that a few of us were at Brucey's house, because it started to become a neighbourhood thing. More of the lads were joining us. Steve was doing his 'Captain's Log' thing for the club video, so had the camcorder out. Soon enough the real thing turned up with local television outside. I don't even know how they got wind of it. It went from a few of us getting together to share in the anxiety, to it becoming something of an impromptu event. And Brucey definitely didn't have a cellar, so God knows where all the booze started to come from. The front garden was full of neighbours.

Oldham won – we were champions. It was a mad evening. We had a game the following day, so we should never have allowed it to get so chaotic. That's the way it happened, though, and I think, when you consider the energy after the Palace game and the way everything bubbled over the following days, the memories are so strong and vivid that this was just our story and the way it unfolded. I don't think I'd change it.

That includes the question: after such a long wait for the club, would you have rather won it on the pitch? By then, though, it was a symbolic moment for everyone. The club itself, the players who'd been before, the present players, the manager, and the supporters who'd been there for so long, waiting for it. Everything unfolding the way it did prolonged the celebrations.

I knew my own celebrations were including a few drinks, so I made my way to and from Old Trafford by taxi the following day. Arriving for the game was crazy. There were so many supporters outside. Usually it would take me 10, 15 minutes to get to the ground. It took an hour, and I felt sorry for the cab driver pulling in right at the top end near where the Munich tunnel is now. The taxi driver was mullered, the car was surrounded.

I remember walking into reception and seeing Kath Phipps. I think she'd joined just after we'd won the league the last time. She'd been waiting longer than anyone. She might have been the happiest person in the whole stadium, but then she had tough competition. I suppose that's the strange thing about not winning it on the pitch. You've spent so long chasing it, and the next day you're at the club and you've done it. There was a sense of disbelief. So this is what it feels like? Everyone is smiling. Hugs all round. An elevated mood and spirit, but it's still a matchday, and you still have your routine. The pre-match meal, it's all so strange, feels so surreal. It's normal, this is what we normally do. Should we do something different now?

The first time that really got embraced was in the dressing room before the game. Our time with the boss, just as the squad. He gave us our congratulations. And then he brought us back down to earth. A bit of a bollocking – the party was a bit of a no-no to put it lightly. But it's the hairdryer with a smile today. He reminds us about the supporters celebrating. We've got a game of football to win. Don't let them down now. Help them continue the party all day. All night. All week.

The problem was that we were still a bit the worse for wear. There was a carnival waiting for us out on the pitch. It was our last home game, so these fans would see the trophy lifted. We were sluggish. Kevin Gallacher grabbed an early goal for Blackburn. Giggsy equalised with a brilliant free kick, the sort of special goal for a special occasion. But we couldn't get going after that. We got to half-time, waited for the boss, and he tore us to bits. The party was mentioned again but this time his tone suggested he wasn't joking. We were letting the fans down. 'They've come here to celebrate with you, they can't celebrate off a performance like that, and they won't be able to celebrate properly, if you go and perform like that again and lose this game.' Words as paracetamol; the anger of the boss as a quick hangover cure. I wouldn't recommend it, as it goes. Incey scored, we could relax.

I'd had a bet on with Pally at the start of the season that I'd score more goals than him. He'd scored one in the previous season and I was so confident I could outscore him that I'd put £100 on the line. There were 40,447 supporters in the ground, add a couple of hundred extra for the teams and the staff and ground staff, and I reckon after 89 minutes I might have even edged Kath out as the happiest man in the stadium with a nice £100 coming my way. Then we get a free kick. Pally goes up and has a conversation, and I thought it was a bit of a joke, but then I saw Incey egging him on. I thought Ince wanted to take it at first. But he steps aside, lets Pally prepare. The Blackburn players must have thought the same as me, that they were taking the piss. But then Pally scores, and for a moment – and I'm joking, I might add – I've gone from the happiest to the man most likely to sulk for a bit. We knew at least we'd survived another blast from the boss and I might have given the hundred for that.

Danny McGregor, the commercial manager, gave us all these white shirts to wear on the pitch as the cameras followed us around. The thing I remember most from the celebrations was being given small replicas of the actual Premier League trophy. I recall Brucey's first reaction: 'It's a fucking darts trophy!' but I think we all loved them. It's absolutely beautiful, one of a kind.

In the early 2000s I was contacted by someone who wanted to buy it. He said a figure – it made my eyes open, but I had to say no. 'If it was Eric's,' he said, 'I'd offer him three times more!' Thanks for that, pal. I get it though. I think that could be a reflection of Eric's importance to that title win for us. It was, still, a win for us all. That was shown in our last game of the season. It was another red invasion down at Selhurst Park. An occasion, an event, that just happened to have a football match as part of the proceedings. One outfield player hadn't scored all season, and it was a player you might not expect – Bryan Robson. He finally had the league championship medal he deserved so much, after 12 years at the club. He got the goal he deserved too, and what a great goal it was. A typical Robbo goal. It wasn't contrived; Robbo wouldn't have had it that way. It wasn't a case of Robbo has to score, but his goal did turn out to be the winner, and that was a perfect way to end off an incredible season.

Two nights before that game, Les Sealey (who'd rejoined the club in January) dragged me out for a celebratory drink on the back of everything. The day after, we got the team bus down to London. I was near the back of the bus and Les was further towards the front. The boss was walking towards the back and I thought he was going to sit down in his usual place, but he stopped at me and gave me a big slap around the back of my head.

'Don't you ever dare go out two nights before a game,' he yells.

I was startled; didn't know what to say. I just watched him march down the bus and do exactly the same to Les.

'Boss …' I started, thinking I could try to reason with him.

'Boss, yeah,' he goes. 'I know all the excuses … you're thinking, how do I know? Well, next time you go into anywhere, always check that no one has anything to do with me. Because my window cleaner saw you, and you know what these people are like, don't you?'

Thankfully that one came with a smile.

12

The Boss is Always Right

AS A professional footballer, you live life in the public eye, but it's elevated to another level when you play for Manchester United. Suddenly you get invitations to meet important people – you end up in situations you'd never have even contemplated. One of those occasions came in the pre-season of 1993 when we went to South Africa and met Nelson Mandela. Mandela had been a huge figure in world news in the months and years prior to our going there and attended our game against the Kaiser Chiefs. We ended up getting a picture with him as a team. It all went over my head. If I'm being fair to myself, I'll say it was all just a bit strange, a bit much. If I'm being critical of myself, I'd say everything was kind of blasé. I thought, *I can do that again another time if I want.* I kind of never really grabbed it as I should have done, or how I wish I'd done. I wish I'd taken that moment, that opportunity, and asked for an individual moment with the man.

I do have to be fair to myself and say everything was so much, a lot to take in. I was in awe of this beautiful country, one I knew I'd have to revisit. We spent most of our time around Johannesburg and were told about the areas that were safe and unsafe. You didn't want to venture out of the bubble you were in due to security concerns, but where we were staying everything was internal to the resort so there was no need to go outside anyway. We went to this bar called Rattlesnakes. The queue was big – as we got closer to the front, we saw this sign above the entrance. If you have guns, please hand them in here. I remember laughing because we thought it was a joke. But we started hearing these loud noises, guns being thrown down on the table to hand them in. *He's got a fucking gun. That's a fucking gun.* Wasn't funny anymore. We were with a few Arsenal players, because they were on the tour with us. I think that was an eye-opening experience for all of us. I don't think I've ever been in a bar where everyone was so well behaved. It was something that I've never witnessed before in my life, at that given time. I wouldn't imagine I'd want to experience or witness anything like it again.

We played Kaiser Chiefs. It sounds mad, doesn't it? Not the pop band. They had one player in midfield. His name was Doctor Khumalo, who I can compare in the way he played to Martin Ødegaard. He kept going round in circles. Every time he had space, and he had a lot of it, he'd suddenly do keepy-uppies. He'd drag the ball back with no one around him, and we effectively just dropped off because there was a little bit of an altitude there. It was their winter, but it was like 70 degrees. But that's one of the funny things as well. At the hotel pool, we'd all be sitting outside having a beer. The staff wouldn't come out and serve us because they said it was too cold, so we'd have to go in. They'd bring us in at the window, they'd wave, and we'd bring the beers out because they said it was too cold. Anyway. I digress. The boss went crazy at half-time when we played that game against the spinning doctor. *Your fitness this, your fitness that*, and I remember Robbo was trying to say, 'Boss, they're doing nothing. We're just sitting back because they're doing nothing. They want to do tricks.' Their fans were going mad, and all we were doing was nicking the ball off of them, and it was just like charge of the light brigade. That's what it was like. We were just going off and banging, hitting them on counters rather than chase around. I obviously had many pre-seasons, but South Africa is probably the most memorable, and a large part of that is for Doctor Khumalo as much as it is for Nelson Mandela.

We had a new face on the tour with us. Roy Keane. I knew of Roy, that he was a good talent, but I have to admit he wasn't somebody who crossed my mind before we signed him. He was a good lad, fitted straight in. On the tour he got drunk. Whenever we went out and he'd had a few, all he'd say was, 'I'm fucking smashed.' So at one point in those early days his nickname was Smashy or Smash. But he was a good lad, and it was a good trip. The only odd thing for me was that Arsenal were on it. We played them in a friendly and then had to play them in the Charity Shield.

Under George Graham, Arsenal had won both domestic cups in 1993. Liverpool were in the early part of their decline, and it was probably the first time that this was understood after them being so successful for so long. Arsenal had won two league titles recently and now we were top dogs, both of us looking to take the place of Liverpool as the dominant team. Blackburn Rovers would emerge as the main challengers that season but I'd have to say that, in the summer, it was very much the case that Arsenal looked as though they'd be best placed.

It was my first Charity Shield. Eyes were on the game looking for either team to get an edge. But it was still pre-season. I think there's too much pressure on everything because you're being judged straight away, and as a player you've got enough issues already rather than being judged when you're supposedly not fit and the game doesn't matter. The main thing about it is the minutes under the belt, getting out there and just getting back into the system of football, getting back into it. When you play those games, you still want your full 90 minutes. You still want to be out there so you can actually feel yourself, your fitness, rather than getting subbed on or subbed off. We won on penalties. I don't think it proved anything.

It was the last game in England before squad numbers came in. There wasn't any big drama as far as I was concerned. I was given No.2, and that was it. My training kit was 48. Some players today have their initials on their training kits! It was all a bit cosmetic at the time. In the future it would become a commercial avenue, but it just wasn't that important back then.

What was important was how we prepared for defending the title. It was an anxious time, at least for me. At Manchester United you're there to be shot at, and that's doubly so if you're at United and you've won the league. If we weren't going to get it on the pitch, we were going to get it from the dressing room from the boss, because the boss was making us aware that we'd done something very difficult in winning a league title but it was going to be even more difficult to retain it, to play as a champion. A lot of people don't understand that. I was fortunate enough to have done it. Players have done it a lot more often than me and been in that position but everyone will say the same thing about when you actually go out there. It's tougher for you personally because you're trying your best, first and foremost, to live up to what you've done before, but you want to go beyond. You want to improve, to do something different to what you've done before, and sometimes, a lot of times, that's the wrong thing to do because there's a reason why you're a champion. You've played in a team full of champions, because you've got everything right and you're trying to change your game, because you think you're different now. But you're not, you're the same person. The only thing that's really changed is that you've got fractionally older from that time of winning to when you're starting again, but it's a different feeling. People talk about it when they have no experience in the matter. I'm sure you can all think of one or two prominent pundits who are quick to talk about the demands of playing for a championship-winning side without having actually having done it themselves. Or the demands of playing for Manchester United without having done that either, all the while never noticing the irony in those very people being the ones creating the noise and the pressure they talk about United players having to live up to.

I think we lived up to that pressure. Well, the proof is in the results. The players around me grabbed hold of it. They seemed to love that control, which came from that feeling. They embraced it and they were still leading each other through situations when they weren't right, but the difference of when you turned up as Manchester United to away games, and you turned up as champions when before you were chasing it ... everyone knew it, and they were working so hard to stop it, because they didn't want to maybe be that team we beat to turn the corner. Then you go back there as a champion and you suddenly find this is just as difficult, this is just as hard, maybe even harder, because they want to beat you as a champion. In my first season at United, the intensity of travelling to away games was something I never really had before but then it was incredible to see there could be a difference again, and an increase in intensity.

People suddenly become a little bit angrier. Where before you'd make a good strong block tackle with somebody, and you get up and you smile, pat each other on the back because you've both gone at it the right way, and haven't tried to hurt each other ... you suddenly find that same player is going in with more intensity because he was being driven on by the fans who wanted to beat Manchester United. There was that different vibe and the boss warned us of it because he'd done it as a manager with Aberdeen.

We started well. We won at Norwich and against Sheffield United, where Smash scored two on his debut. Then we played Newcastle, who'd just come up from the First Division – they gave it everything and didn't stop even when we took the lead. Andy Cole scored to get them a point. It was a handy reminder of how hard teams would try against us, and the boss wasn't happy with that performance before we went to Villa Park.

It's a distinctive game for me because we played in the popular all-black strip for the first time. It was a big test for us so early in the season to go to our biggest contenders from the previous year. Sharpey scored twice and we won 2-1. Everyone was on a high after that because that was a test and we played with so much confidence.

We played brilliantly in wins over Southampton and West Ham and then we started to get compliments in the press from former great players. George Best, Denis Law and Bobby Charlton, the Holy Trinity, all three were often interviewed by the press or on television and they'd say nice things about the way we were playing. It invites comparisons because people want to then talk about the different teams from different eras, not because they want to celebrate in the press, but because the newspapers want to have something ready to throw at you if it doesn't work out. Looking at it the other way, I know the conditions those players had to play in and what they had to endure leading into games, and I could compare that to what I had. They were just a great side in that era and you can't compare them to any other Manchester United side. It was a different kind of football.

I can still remember watching United in their relegation season when I was a kid. I can remember the following year more than the relegation season because that was something unbelievable. It was people talking about Manchester United now as a Second Division team. You suddenly saw what United had – they were renowned for their great size but the promotion team wasn't about size or glamour. It was about fight. Even the relegated team, they had a fight about them. There was a never-say-die spirit. Everything was given and this squad of 13 or 14 players, they had to give everything. And they did. Spirit and quality are two very different things, and you have to have both if you want to be remembered. The promotion team were very fondly remembered, as much as the 1968 side in some eyes.

To even begin to live up to being worthy of the words of legends, we felt we'd have to make our own history. The first obvious step towards that would be in the European Cup. We were drawn against Kispest Honvéd in the first round. Hungary had been a global powerhouse of football but was something of a sleeping giant in the early 90s and, speaking for myself, maybe I took them for granted a little. I quickly realised that you couldn't rest for a minute. You were never comfortable. They were the best in their country and knew their strengths; they could catch you off-guard and one unexpected moment could completely change the pattern of a tie. The boss warned us about it. Don't ever trust it. Something will happen. It was a different standard of competition. We got through the tie with Honvéd but had a few of those hiccups to navigate, and I can say that my own naivety and inexperience in Europe might not have helped, but I felt we'd learned enough of a lesson in that tie to warn us against switching off in the future.

Confidence can be a double-edged sword. We were playing so well and beating teams at a canter but conceding a few goals in the process. When things are going as swimmingly as they were it can be difficult to maintain a competitive edge, and that's a lesson for life, really. You can become overconfident. Too much belief in the other players that something will happen, and you'll get out of whatever problem you might find yourself in. From someone who played in an overachieving side at Queens Park Rangers and how we did in the big games – you work so hard for every moment in the game and know that you can't give a sniff of a chance because you can be two goals up and switch off for a second and the momentum completely goes. But when you're at one of those top clubs and you're winning by a couple, and it happens as often as it was doing for us, then you start to feel almost invincible.

We were 2-0 up against Galatasaray at Old Trafford. These Turkish players were in the biggest game of their lifetime and they weren't going to just give up after 13 minutes. They pulled it back to 2-2 before half-time, and it does change everything. Their fans become inspired to be even noisier. Your own get a little agitated. You can feel it coming from the terraces. You half-wonder whether there's something going on you don't know about. They went 3-2 up early in the second half. We were lucky that the player we turned to in that situation, Eric, got us out of it on the night. The 3-3 draw salvaged a result but not our blushes, and the events of the game would prove costly.

If we'd gone to Turkey for the second leg with that 2-0 advantage, it would have been a different game and we'd have experienced a completely different atmosphere.

They'd have been intense, it would have been aggressive and uncompromising, but we'd have a safety net and they wouldn't have all the belief they'd earned from their fightback.

We arrived at the airport to the scenes everybody has witnessed – the Galatasaray fans at arrivals, the big signs saying 'Welcome to Hell'. We stayed at a beautiful old hotel. It was so peaceful. The staff couldn't do enough. They had shoe cleaners and you had to force them to take money from you. It was as though they just wanted the privilege of cleaning the shoes of Manchester United's players. Everyone was extremely nice.

On the day of the game it was as though someone had whipped them up into a frenzy and told them they must hate, with a passion, anything and everything connected with Manchester United. It was tangible. It was very, very volatile. Those same staff who'd been so welcoming ... well, if I say they made us feel like unwelcome guests, I'd be putting it politely. We had a really good police escort in to the stadium; we needed it to get in there. We got out on to the pitch to be welcomed by a quadraphonic sound of this song they were singing. It was just going all around the stadium a good two hours before kick-off. I hadn't witnessed anything like it. Nobody had. It was just something incredible. And it was brilliant, the way everything was in sequence.

But then the game started and we learned of the hostility towards us. Whistles every time we were on the ball, again pervading every corner of the stadium. The referee was absolutely dreadful. The game was constantly stopping. The atmosphere was something I'd never witnessed during my career and never did again, but the referee seemed to be caught up in it. I think the atmosphere affected some of his decisions. We couldn't get going. It was like watching the game today really, with the referee often stopping the game. Every physical incident was followed by a home player screaming and falling to the ground, and the referee's whistle. It was as though there had been a collusion and an agreement we weren't aware of – no football to be played today. The number of times he stopped it, there should have been a minimum of 15 minutes added on. I don't even think we had two.

It felt as though we were constantly on the verge of physical conflict. It could be the tackles on the pitch or even when you went to take a throw-in. I'd feel conscious about what was going on behind me, more worried about that than where I'd throw the ball. I think the referee made it worse by giving all the needless decisions. A stronger referee helps the game flow and also helps to calm the atmosphere, or at least doesn't make it worse. Football might have won through. We'd have had a different game. Having said that, we didn't put ourselves in a good position because of the performance in the first leg. We drew 0-0. Out.

After the game, Eric was livid, and argued with the referee. He was given a red card. The security and police crowded around us and we were effectively pushed off the pitch. There were steps going back down to the changing rooms. We were getting pushed and shoved as we were walking down. I got shoved in the back, and it was only big Pete that stopped me going down the concrete steps. I nearly went head-first down. If it had been anyone other than Pete they might have dislocated their shoulder.

The boss was angry. Seriously, seriously angry. It seemed as though it was anger at a few things, but in the moment he was more concerned about safety and about us getting out of the ground. So it was a case of grabbing everything we had, no showers, get on the coach. There was no security, it was just aggressive, it was awful. We had to go through the crowds of supporters throwing all sorts of things at the coach. I was sitting on the other side to Brucey, who was lucky that the brick that was thrown at the window didn't go through it and hit him in the face. We finally got on to some open road and allowed ourselves a sigh of relief. The coach drove into the airport, basically on to the runway, but we could see plenty of Galatasaray fans had got into the airport and were outside the fences, baiting us, making a racket. Even when we were sitting on the plane, they were still there. It was difficult enough being knocked out without that misery. It was a tough flight.

Maybe the best thing for us was that we had a big game waiting for us back at home. The biggest story was United being knocked out of the Champions League. Glorification of our pain. It didn't matter that we were novices in the competition, that we were representing England. We were reviled by the opposition and hated even by our own press. Defeat for Manchester United is success and celebration for everybody else. We had Manchester City at Maine Road. As we came out of the tunnel we were pelted by Turkish Delight.

Sweet. They scored twice, through Niall Quinn. As we went back to the tunnel, I was getting sick of them. Steve McMahon was winding up his own fans. Punching the air. I recall it clearly. He's having a go about it and, again, it dawns on me the real hate from Liverpudlians, you know, for Manchester United, because it was massive to him to be doing what he was doing. You'd have thought, really, your common sense would kick in and say wait until the end of the game.

The entrances to the changing rooms at Maine Road had two doors, one leading out on to the pitch, but the one you entered through was from the front of the ground. We all went through and were sitting down waiting for the boss. He went berserk, as expected. He went to open the other door and at that very moment the actor Warren Clark, famous for his role in *Dalziel and Pascoe*, was walking past. The boss grabbed him and virtually dragged him into the room.

'You go in there,' he says to Clarke, 'and you fucking sort these fuckers out.'

Warren stood there for a second. He was quiet. So were we. Stunned, really.

'I don't know what I'm supposed to do,' he eventually says. 'I'm a blue!'

Kiddo, ever the pacifier, took the sting out of the situation. Sorry about that Warren, mate. Kiddo talked to us. He was a bit softer on us than the boss. Eric was told to drop a bit deeper on the instruction of the boss. It was an incredible second half. Early on, David White should have scored to make it 3-0, and it was as though that chance rang an alarm bell. They were on fire, the City lads, but maybe too pumped up. Terry Phelan was giving it large. Keith Curle thought he could outrun everyone. When Eric dropped a bit deeper, his calmness and football intelligence shifted the momentum in our direction. Had it stayed 2-0, it would have been a critical result in the season, not just for City.

We'd learned the hard way that over-confidence leads to silly mistakes. Vonk made one with a backwards header. Eric was lurking, and scored to bring us back into it. Everyone remembers his second goal, where he was juggling the ball and then Ryan played the sort of ball that only he could, for Eric to tap in at the back post. There was only one winner then. Roy Keane scored the decisive goal right at the end – he'd already scored a fair few for us in his first couple of months, but this was a big, big goal, and earned us a memorable and crucial win. It took us to 58 points from the last 63 available. When you play so many games over a career, the ebbs and flows of individual matches are sometimes hard to recall, but that's one that always sticks out.

We were ticking along nicely. We played nice football in wins over Wimbledon, Sheffield United, Aston Villa and Oldham before New Year, and when we needed to show the sort of spirit we'd demonstrated in that win over Sheffield Wednesday, it came in the form of a last-gasp equaliser from Paul Ince on Boxing Day against Blackburn, who'd emerged as our closest challengers. Challengers felt like it was probably generous – they had a game in hand over us at the turn of the year, but were 14 points behind.

They were counting on complacency from us. Despite how well we'd played throughout the season, that was a word that was haunting us and pushing us on. I couldn't attribute our dropped points in the next two games to complacency. We drew 0-0 with Leeds, who were well-drilled by their manager Howard Wilkinson. We drew 3-3 at Anfield in a game that could hardly have been more different.

We went 3-0 up. Brucey scored and then Giggsy and Denis struck superb goals. But Anfield has a thing, and teams have found that out against United in their post-Sir Alex years too, that rarely can you completely relax, because you're playing against a team and you're also playing against a club. Anfield is a place for it – you just can't relax. A single goal can transform the atmosphere, and it did, when Nigel Clough scored, out of nothing really. Clough scored again before half-time and the second half they just didn't stop going for that point. It eventually came through Neil Ruddock's header, and if you want to know how much it meant to them, rewatch that goal and the force with which he comes in. These days there's every chance the referee will give a foul in a situation like that because the momentum of you coming in and heading it! It was an incredibly brave header. Not many teams go to Anfield and go 3-0 up, even in their more difficult days, and we were frustrated to have let it slip. It would rightly go down as one of the great Premier League games, and that's how the boss talked about it with his public face, but in the dressing room he went ballistic.

The boss laid a lot of blame for that result specifically on Peter. Peter isn't the best at handling that sort of criticism and, let's be fair, it's also a very particular circumstance, and nobody would enjoy it. We may all say we can take criticism. Nobody enjoys it, though. In that situation it's like being in a boxing match and you're being pummelled. Don't even bother lifting your gloves up to hit back. The boss is always right. You quell your ego. It's difficult. You're taking it big time, in front of your team-mates. What you should do is what Brian McClair always did. 'Yeah, you're right. You're right boss.' And the boss would still be fuming, probably even wound up, but what else can he do? 'Yeah, I shouldn't have done that. I should have done it exactly like you're saying boss.' You couldn't laugh. Choccy was dry, and in any other situation you couldn't help *but* laugh, but you'd just hope it would be over before the boss blew a fuse. Pete, though, on this occasion, decided to ignite it. He bit back. 'It's not my fault. I'm right.' You're never right with the boss, even if you are right, even if we all agree with you.

In another game the boss had questioned the position I took up. He said I was too high and was relying on my pace to get me out of trouble. I argued back and said, no, I was in the right place. It had been a half where I was playing down by the North Stand, and the way the pitch goes at Old Trafford there was a slight bow on it, so it affects your view slightly. I thought I could argue the point and get away with it. No shouting or screaming, really, just a minor disagreement – or so I thought. He goes, 'Well, come and see me tomorrow morning at 7am.'

I already regretted it, having to go in on my day off. I went in to The Cliff, into his office, and the boss welcomed me in with a beaming smile on his face. He flicked his VHS on and sat back on his chair, not saying a single word. Just nodding at me to watch. So I did. I could feel his eyes on me. I finally looked at him and he had a big grin on his face. He was right, of course. Obviously. I shrugged my shoulders. 'Yeah, okay, sorry boss.'

He asked me what I was going to do. Was I going to have a bit of breakfast before I went home? I said, 'Yeah, I might as well.' Other people were in and around. They all asked what I was doing in. They knew I'd been in the room of doom. They knew I'd been battered without being touched, without so much as a single word. Hadn't even needed to note anything down, didn't try to look clever.

Peter's stand of defiance led both him and the boss to say he should leave the club. But then he came down to the rest of us and said sorry before our next training session. The boss apparently heard him, and changed his mind. Peter was grateful for that, and we all would have been too, if we'd known how close that had come. The first we knew about it was when Peter released his first autobiography. In his second, he expressed regret about sharing the story of the row in the first place. The sanctuary of the dressing room is real, but this was a great example – you could be the greatest in your position in the world, as Peter was, and things could be going as well as possible, but nobody was bigger than the boss at Manchester United.

13
A United Bond

IN JANUARY 1994, Sir Matt Busby passed away. I never had any real interactions with him, no conversations. I wish I had. At the time, I might have been too nervous. But he wasn't always around. He wasn't a Bill Shankly, hanging around the training ground. Bobby Charlton would be the one we'd see quite often. Bobby still wanted to be one of the lads in a sense; he still hadn't got it out of his system and I think everyone saw that in the fact that he used to come and have a kickabout with us on the nights before European games. We loved it. He joined in with the banter, but we still knew there was a line not to cross: Sir Bobby, or Mr Charlton, never just Bobby.

I'm talking about Sir Matt but I can't help but draw parallels with the experience I had in early 2025 when Kath Phipps, the long-serving receptionist at the club, sadly passed away. At Kath's funeral I bumped into Ken Ramsden and called him Mr Ramsden. 'My name's Ken, Paul,' he laughed. It just wasn't me. I was mesmerised in Manchester Cathedral. Jonny Evans gave a lovely speech. There were players across multiple generations and staff just the same. It was a lovely service and it's difficult to envisage that in any other business or walk of life, where football and community become part of the same thing. We were all there because Kath meant something to us, she was part of the club, a big part, and it illustrated to me that you could be the receptionist or a legendary manager, and you'd be treated with similar reverence by those who shared some of their life with you.

I'd only been at the club for a relatively short time when Sir Matt passed away. From the outside you know the story about the success and rebuilding the club after Munich, but it's when you get inside and you learn more about what went into that recovery. I don't think many people could say otherwise, and I'm speaking from the point of view of being a professional footballer, but I was just an ordinary person who knew about a football club because I played the game, then when I went to the club, I grabbed the history of United a lot more than I did any other club I played for. I found that I wanted to be perfect, I didn't want to let anybody down. I wanted to know everything. I'm glad that I did do that, because I don't think there's any other way you can be when you're playing for Manchester United. You could be anywhere, and someone will want to talk about the club and the history, and I think if you were a bit naive, I don't think it would go down too well.

Even playing in European football is different – okay, so I didn't experience it anywhere *but* Old Trafford, but when you play in a continental competition for United, you're following a proud heritage, you become part of that lineage, and when you go overseas and see the opposition clubs and fans, no matter what country they're in, there's a respect associated with the club. Even now, decades after I retired, no matter where I am in the world, there are people who connect me to the club, and yes, that's the reputation of the club, but I can't disassociate it with the tradition of the club that was started by Sir Matt.

I was very fortunate that I made my greatest-ever football decision in signing for Manchester United. If I'd made a money decision, then I'd have been playing in London. But I couldn't help but be drawn, I couldn't help think of my dad, who was just a big George Best, Denis Law, Bobby Charlton fan. Not a United fan. He ended up an Arsenal fan, as it goes. But he had a thing for that United team.

Everything in life that has happened to me in football since 1991 is because of Manchester United. Everything at United goes back to Matt Busby. I heard about his passing on the news. Because I didn't know him personally, I didn't really know how to feel, but you could feel the sadness all around. Everyone at the club went automatically into a state of mourning, and you become respectful and then become affected by it too. You automatically think that's a Manchester United thing but quickly realise it's a Manchester thing. It's about the city itself. There were people all around Manchester, and all around the country, too, who felt a tremendous sadness. A member of everybody's family had passed away.

Life is different now. There's so much information and there's a readiness to celebrate people when they pass, in acknowledgement for everything they achieved. I'm not making a comment on whether or not that's appropriate, it's just a comment on the way life changes – it just wasn't that way in the early 90s. There was only sadness and respect. It was a huge event at the club. Now, when I look back at it, I wonder with some anxiety whether I conducted myself in the right fashion.

We were told that before our next game – which was against Everton at Old Trafford a couple of days after Sir Matt passed away – that there would be a procession before kick-off, with a piper leading us out. My memory of it all was that the boss was central to the arrangements, he was at the point of command.

Forgive me for switching back and forth between 1994 and 2025, because I can't help but think of the boss giving a speech at Kath's funeral. He said words to the effect of it only being possible that a football club could be run properly by a football manager. I was surrounded by players across generations, many of whom I'd played with, plenty who I hadn't. Giggs, Scholesy, Roy, Nev, were all in front of me. Russell Beardsmore and Lee Martin were nearby. Lou Macari, too. When the boss said that, I could feel every single former player nodding their heads in agreement.

He talked about when he met Kath. She'd already been at the club close to 20 years by the time he got the job as manager. He said if there was ever anything he needed, Kath would be his point of contact. Literally anything, he'd make a call from The Cliff and get through to Kath.

When I arrived, I was self-conscious about annoying the boss with little queries – literally just the little things about settling in – and I learned pretty quickly that Robbo could be cutting if he felt it was a silly question. You'd have no way of knowing what was a silly question, but you'd find out if Robbo thought so, because you'd get the piss ripped out of you for ages. Pop had this way of letting things out. You could ask him something and think it was perfectly reasonable, and he'd let you think so too, but then you'd get in front of an audience and he had a way of letting it out, keeping a perfectly straight face … it was incredible, you'd feel demoralised, and you'd want to throw something at him. So it forced me to go to the boss instead and I got a lot of 'fucking this, fucking that', which made me wonder whether I'd get out of the office alive. You wouldn't want to annoy him for risk of being dropped. So I stopped doing that too. When we returned to Old Trafford after training, we'd all pop into reception and Kath would be there with her colleagues. I remember the first time I asked her something and she asked whether I'd asked the boss. Her reaction to my nod: 'Oh, he hasn't got much patience, has he?'

That turned from requests to conversations, to chats with a hug. She'd always have your mail organised for you and it got to be that Kath became another person you didn't want to annoy. You didn't want to leave it too long.

'Where've you been?'

'The Cliff!'

'Before that? You haven't been in here since …'

Then you'd get a clip, not because you've let stuff pile up, but because you haven't been to see her. I remember the first time I came back, years after retiring, after I'd lived in

Singapore, the first person I saw when I came back for a game was Kath.

'Where have you been?'

'Singapore!' I said, thinking it was a good enough answer.

'Oh, I knew you were abroad,' she replied. 'You didn't want to keep in touch?'

And I laughed and thought, *You know what, Kath, you're right. I should have done.* She had warmth. She was the reason, to me, that Manchester United was such a welcoming place.

So, the Everton game. It was a difficult experience. One of the most difficult games to play in, and I say that as a United player. Ian Snodin was playing for Everton that day. I can vividly remember our conversation after the match. 'We were shit,' he admitted, 'but I found it hard to play because of what was going on ... I'm sure the other lads felt it, we didn't want to ruin the day, and it felt like there was something stopping us.'

We won 1-0. It was haunting to be led on to the pitch by the piper. The silence in the ground was immaculate. The atmosphere was strange. The supporters tried. But it was an occasion, and it was real, and everything that was surrounding the game made its way into the game. Ryan scored our goal. We had chances but couldn't score again. You can't really celebrate on a day like that. Normally you'd go and shake your opponent's hands, have a chat, but you didn't want to be seen to be smiling, you didn't want to be disrespectful for fear of it being taken the wrong way.

We played some of our very best football in the weeks after Sir Matt passed away. Most people remember the Wimbledon game in the FA Cup, a game where they tried to kick the crap out of us. You watch that game and think about some of the things that went on, but it was just one of those days where you could see from our reactions that we weren't going to take it. Eric used to run in a way that he seemed to be bouncing on his toes. One of the worst challenges was from Vinnie Jones on Eric. It was fortunate that Eric glided the way he did. He must have felt or foreseen something, and he managed to get his feet off the floor, because that kind of challenge was the one that leaves your foot in the ground, and you need to either go back to the changing room or to hospital. He did one on Keano as well. Keane just got up and gave him that look, which is quite scary, a summing-up kind of calculating look that Keano's got, just logging it in the back of his head, because he's got one heck of a memory. All of us got some kind of kick, me included, and I just resolved to win the ball back as firmly as I could.

That was a game that summed up our different qualities, but to me it was a 90-minute example of our honesty and selflessness when it came to each other. You don't shirk your responsibilities, you don't shirk a tackle, and you don't shirk on your team-mates. Everyone runs for each other, whatever problem there is, while you're on that pitch – there's no problem. That was instilled more than anything by Robbo, and he wasn't even playing. I know that every team will come out and say similar things, but there was that different feeling during that period with that team where, first and foremost, you felt invincible as a football team, and you did often feel fear from other teams when you played. There was always that side of it, you could see it in them, especially when the ball started moving. Every pass was progressive. We were fearless in the fact that we were trying to do things without fear of losing the ball.

Wimbledon had a good cup team and were used to getting a little bit of the headlines themselves. They wanted more, and they didn't care about how they got them. They were quite open about it. Football is about adulation and being in the limelight, every player wants it, every team wants it as well. They'd threatened to give us a hard time. We stood up to it, and just before half-time Eric scored the sort of incredible goal that only he could. Flicked it up and volleyed it in. You can't win the fight and you can't win the game. Incey scored. Den scored one of the greatest goals you can see from a team and a full-back. It was the most comprehensive 3-0 you could ever see.

So many qualities were on show in that run. Ryan was electric – he scored goals against Sheffield Wednesday in the League Cup semi-final and against QPR in the league, which had people once more comparing him to George Best. Even when we were on the verge of defeat, we had something – usually Paul Ince, as it had been at Blackburn, and again at West Ham when he was getting abuse from the home fans. He loved that. Revelled in it. Got our equaliser just before the end. That stretched our unbeaten run to 33 games. We made it 34 and got through to the final of the League Cup, battering Wednesday 4-1 at Hillsborough.

Eric missed that game with a knock and he was out of our home game against Chelsea. All good things come to an end, and Chelsea repeated their feat of earlier in the season and won 1-0. What did they have that other teams didn't? Apparently, Gavin Peacock. It wouldn't be the last we'd see of him. Sometimes you come up against teams who just have a way to beat you and it does become a mental test. Prior to joining United, I never won against Crystal Palace. I started to wonder if I ever would.

At Stamford Bridge the closest we'd come to scoring had been through a remarkable effort from Eric – he'd tried a half-volley on the turn from near the halfway line. It bounced and hit the bar. Chelsea broke and scored almost immediately through Gavin. When he scored just after the hour at Old Trafford, you start to feel that sense of draining. I was brought off for Dion Dublin. We just couldn't find a goal.

I must admit that it had started to feel a little more hostile since our Turkish experience. We'd played Norwich in the FA Cup in the round before we went to Wimbledon and even that had been an aggressive match against one of the teams you could consider to be one of the pure footballing outfits. Then there had been the match at West Ham. We bounced back from the loss against Chelsea by beating Charlton in the cup and putting in one of our strongest performances against Sheffield Wednesday, before we went to Swindon, the bottom team in the league.

They were doomed anyway, and we were champions elect – not quite yet sure enough to consider it inevitable – and we found Swindon to be one of those sides who were desperate to make a name for themselves and be talked about more in the light of their association with interrupting our success rather than their own ambitions. So came the kicking. Look, I won't complain about that. We could physically match any team who wanted to do that, maybe even surpass some of them. I mean, as much as our team had great footballers, they had a side to them that could always change.

The boss was more concerned about players losing their heads than he was worried about them being kicked, because he knew if they were being kicked, they were going to deal with it themselves. It was almost an expectation. You've got to win the battle to win the war – he'd remind us that they were hardly going to let us play lovely football, and then he he'd say, 'If you think that, you shouldn't be at this football club.'

But there's aggression and hostility and then there was this moment in time where it just seemed to be a little much. Swindon as a town seemed seriously angry from the moment we arrived. With their all-red strip and their previous insistence on the nice, flowing football that had earned them an incredible promotion, you could have been mistaken for thinking we were in Liverpool by the bitterness that welcomed us. The supporters were wanting to fight us as we got off the coach. You don't expect pats on the back but every single thing that went on that day had this vicious undertone. Every challenge was laced with malice. You couldn't take a throw-in without some form of confrontation. Eventually the flashpoint came when Johnny Moncur – a decent footballer – tried to get too close to Eric, took a swipe, and ended up with Eric's studs in his midriff as a consequence. What Eric did was wrong and he received a red card. But I think every single one of us had felt like doing that at some point in the match. Eric had to deal with that every single game, so rather than say it was a case of him having a shorter fuse, it was more the point that it had been going on for so long and there's only so much to anyone's tolerance levels.

We got a point, a great point, out of that game. If we'd lost there, it would have been a big story, it would have been everything. The game was pretty similar to the Galatasaray game, the difference was this time that the referee had no choice but to stop it, because some of the tackles were a bit malicious. I hadn't played in a game that volatile, with that level of aggression since I was in the Third Division with Fulham.

In those days it would be a couple of weeks until suspensions kicked in. So there was still time for Eric to somehow get sent off again – this time at Arsenal, although he was a bit unlucky at Highbury. It meant he'd have a five-game suspension. Peter Schmeichel had also been sent off against Charlton after he'd rushed outside of the area, so far from us being portrayed as a team who faced aggression, we were seen as the culprits by many.

It wasn't the greatest preparation for our League Cup Final against Aston Villa. Peter was suspended, so Les Sealey was called in to play. Ron Atkinson had won the League Cup against United with Sheffield Wednesday in the season before I joined – and Villa, of course, had something to prove after running us close the previous season. It was a tough game, a rainy day with long grass at Wembley. We just couldn't get going. We went 2-0 down. Hughesie pulled one back, so we bombed forward, but in the last minute they broke and Andrei, in blocking a shot on the line, was sent off for handball. Penalty. 3-1. Game over. And our chance of history, of becoming the first-ever team in England to win the domestic treble, gone with it.

The boss put it down to just one of those days. It was sandwiched between that midweek trip to Arsenal and the visit of Liverpool to Old Trafford in the league a couple of days later. Can you imagine how a modern manager would react with such a schedule?

We put in a decent performance against Liverpool. It was probably the best thing for us. Back on the train, back in training, big game to focus on. Paul Ince scored, we won 1-0. Then three days later we played at Blackburn, our first match with Eric after his red cards. It was flat. I remember being confused when we arrived; Blackburn had been spending big under Jack Walker, but when we got to Ewood Park, we got changed in Portakabins. It was a big game but just lacked the sort of buzz that should come with us. We lost 2-0. They now had a sniff of a chance in the league and the boss was furious. The last thing he wanted to do was lose to Blackburn, managed by Kenny Dalglish, with both goals scored by Alan Shearer, a player the boss had failed to sign. It was a bigger occasion to Blackburn because this was the first time they could really be seen as competitors. To be fair to them, they made a mark on the day and left a message. We were left with a point to prove to ourselves.

14
Our Own Piece of History

AGAINST BLACKBURN, I'd come off with 20 minutes to go, and as much as you could explain it as us chasing a goal again, with Choccy coming on for me, I'd been caught by Kevin Gallacher with a late tackle – that old-fashioned bollocks about forwards not being able to tackle. As I knocked the ball down the line, he just came through late and just hit me on the ankle. The worst thing, I always say, is no one seriously gets injured if your feet are off the floor. It has to be a really, really terrible challenge with a hell of a lot of ferocity to have lasting damage if you're caught like that. But my ankle was planted. It had just come down from knocking the ball down the line and he hit me late. I tried to shrug it off. The old bulldog mentality then was not to show an opponent they'd injured you. I tried to run it off. Even when it started to hurt, I thought long-term I'd be fine. I was hobbling on it and the adrenalin kicked in, but the blood pumps, the pain comes and I knew I had to come off.

The boss left me out completely for the visit of Oldham two days later. I was desperately unhappy to miss that game.

I'd played almost every game throughout the season, we were close to achieving something special, and on top of that it was my birthday.

One thing I didn't do was argue about it. The manager knew I was unhappy and frustrated. He also knew I was taking a lot of painkillers to get through, and not training to the same kind of intensity as usual. The boss gave it the usual 'we're playing a lot of games, you get a breather here because we'll need you at the weekend'. The weekend was Oldham again, in the FA Cup semi-final at Wembley. But there was a lot riding on every game. The boss was right. He didn't want my injury to get aggravated. But I was stubborn and I knew how stiff the competition was at the club. I didn't want to have to take time out and, so close to the season concluding, I didn't even want to entertain the suggestion that I should just take that time to let my ankle recover, even if that might have been the best thing for it.

I can give that opinion blessed with the benefit of hindsight but in the moment you're presented with a dilemma and you have to find your strength from somewhere. My thought was this: how would I feel if we achieved big things and I wasn't involved because of an injury where I might have got away with wearing strappings or having painkillers? I knew I wouldn't feel the same involvement. Importantly, for myself, did I feel I could still do myself justice on the pitch? Did I feel as though I wouldn't let my team-mates down? Yes, I did feel like that, I felt I could push through it. You add all the other bits – playing bonuses, win bonuses, what was on offer in this last ten games or so – and it was too important to miss out on.

The first thing was not missing out on that Wembley date, so I reluctantly accepted the decision of the boss. I was on anti-inflammatories. I needed to be involved. You just can't play at Wembley enough. I'd just lost there. I needed to put that right. The pitch was a little better but it was hard going. Oldham had lost against us at Old Trafford but gave it everything in the semi-final. It went to extra time, and then the second half of extra time, still goalless. Then Oldham scored, and the boss did what he did against Sheffield Wednesday exactly a year to the day earlier and decided that the best difference I could make would be to come off. Nicky Butt came on. Nicky played a role in a frantic last-minute exchange where the ball was hooked into the boss and Sparky scored a dramatic equaliser. Sparky was always a big-game player and that was a typical Mark Hughes goal. You knew he was one that you could always guarantee, when it came to a big game, he was going to have a moment of involvement because he was that kind of player. It was just something, everything about it.

A team like ours comprised players finding their place at all the right times. Sparky had endured difficult times since he'd returned to the club. Prior to my arrival he'd even been dropped a few times. He wasn't a player to score 30 goals a season but he was the man for the big occasion. He'd proved that in the European Cup Winners' Cup Final in 1991. I think, when the pressure was on in 1992, the demand was too great on him to do too many things, but with Eric's arrival both he and Choccy had flourished to play some great football. It's arguable that few players in the club's history had that sense of occasion quite like Sparky.

In the replay at Maine Road we absolutely dominated Oldham. We absolutely wiped them off the park. Irwin and Kanchelskis scored amazing goals in the first few minutes. It was like the football of the winter had returned and it was a big statement of a performance considering we were missing Eric and that so much was centred around him. To be able to go and perform like that, like we did, and Eric not being involved, did say a lot really. I think he'd passed a little bit of his charisma on to us. The media were obviously always on top of it when Eric wasn't playing. They started to question us without him. But I think the team, the club even, had grown in stature and confidence. We were better with him but we were still good enough to be the best without him.

That's not to say he wasn't missed, or that we were invincible without him. A 1-0 defeat at Wimbledon proved that. It was an absolutely horrible game of football. It was a typical Wimbledon occasion – the loud music in the dressing room, the banging on the walls, all ramped up that little bit more because they were desperate for revenge after what had happened in the cup. And they treated it as though they'd won the war. They were delighted by it. We were dragged down to their level.

Thankfully that was the last game of Eric's ban and we had a full week to prepare for the next game, the visit of Manchester City. We were fortunate that we'd come through the wobble and still had an advantage in the league. We could give ourselves excuses but the fact of the matter is we'd lost that air of invincibility we were feeling and we had to get it back. Every manager wants a fit and available squad but the boss this season seemed to want his spine out there every week. Our disappointments had been self-inflicted, but none of us moaned about it. Europe had been a disappointment. So had the League Cup. But we were still within grasp of a historic achievement – winning two major trophies for the first time in the club's history. We were all desperate to play and I think that played a part in the manager's consistent selection. I think he saw it in everybody. He definitely saw in me that I was desperate to play every single game for Manchester United. The worst thing for me was sitting on the bench or not being involved at all because you feel like a spare leg, especially when the team win. So I wanted to be around on that pitch every time we won a game. Even if we lost a game, I wanted to be a part of it, to have that same feeling those other lads did.

Eric's return was predictably triumphant. Two goals, 2-0. City taken care of. Andrei and Ryan then scored in an accomplished win at Elland Road. These were big victories with all of our main players featuring. The press were looking for a wobble or another Eric explosion. He was coolness personified. So were we. We knew we needed two wins from our last three games, and the last two were at home. We went to Ipswich before that and went a goal down. Schmeichel got injured. He'd been complaining about the pitch – it was a horrible surface at Portman Road, surprisingly so for the first day of May. But Eric and Ryan scored in the second half, a flex of our experience, and we were on the verge of winning the title again.

Blackburn had to keep winning to stay in with a chance. They were at Coventry on *Monday Night Football.* A few of us went round to Brucey's, looking to tempt fate again, and the cameras were well aware of it in advance this time. I think that probably helped us indulge a little less, knowing we were being watched. I don't think the boss would have let us get away with it a second time.

Trivia question: what links Ian Olney and Julian Darby? These are the names of the footballers who scored the goals that won Manchester United's first two Premier League titles. Not Eric Cantona, Mark Hughes, Ryan Giggs or even Paul Parker. Just as Olney's strike for Oldham earned them the decisive win over Villa in 1993, now Julian Darby, who I'm led to believe is a Liverpool fan, scored twice for Coventry as they defeated Blackburn 2-1.

My experience of winning the league title again came on Brucey's settee rather than on the pitch. But we'd done the job over the previous 40 league games, playing some exceptional football, and the league is about the full season and not about the glory moment. That's how things work out at a given time. So, yes, those two Premier League titles, those first two Premier League titles, we didn't go out and win a game to win the league. Other teams had gone out and beaten teams who were chasing us. It had been a test, especially during the second half of the season, a real test of physical endurance. We'd stayed the course. It's just strange, one of those things, that Oldham and Coventry were the teams we had to thank for those first two wins happening when they did.

We played Southampton in midweek, which wasn't quite the carnival Blackburn had been, but was a celebration nonetheless. The dressing rooms had been moved and the tunnel to the pitch now came out from the corner of the Stretford End. I loved the change. I loved the tunnel in the middle as well – the history that was attached to it. But I enjoyed the change, the longer walk, I think it made it more difficult for our opponents. We won against Southampton, 2-0.

The last game was against Coventry. That week, Bryan Robson had announced to us that he'd be leaving. There had been rumours. He'd been on the coaching staff of Terry Venables, the new England manager, for a few months. He was linked with becoming player-manager of Wolves. Robbo was a good card player. We had a gut feeling he was going but he never responded to the speculation or discussed it. He was the captain of Manchester United, and even when Steve Bruce held the armband because he played more regularly, Robbo always conducted himself as the skipper and led by example. So there was the air that it was his last year with us and I remember more than once thinking, wishing, that the season could go on a little longer, just so we'd get more time with him.

I don't think I was alone. He was going to be missed on the pitch just as much as he was off it, because he was a big presence off the pitch. A lot of people would say that's an easy thing to say, but this isn't faint praise – there hasn't really been a captain like Bryan Robson. Perhaps Roy came close. I wasn't at the club when Roy was skipper, and I'd still argue he'd have been influenced in his leadership skills by Robbo. Robbo was in a different league. Captains are nowhere near what Bryan Robson was. It just doesn't work out that way. Society is never going to allow that again because someone like him, a player, a person to lead people to war, they're not bred.

Captains today lead by show and not by example. A lot of them shout and point. Robbo wasn't there to do things for the cameras. If the ball went for a throw-in, Robbo would get the ball for you. He'd bring it to you, give it to you and he'd talk to you. And he'd smile and laugh while he's calling you a wanker for not doing something, or telling you to do your effing job. But he'd smile and no one would know that he's having a go at you. If you let Robbo down it was worse than letting the boss down.

His relationship with the boss was incredible. You're just not going to get a manager having a relationship with someone who's a captain and someone who, when the manager turned up, was already captain as well. He kept him there. Trusted him. And everything was run through that way. The relationship was absolutely incredible. The respect between them both … wow. Every time you saw Robbo speaking with the boss, straight away you wanted to go and ask the question. *What's going on?* At some point he'd come out and you'd be told. But he wasn't one of them who goes 'the boss has said this, the boss has said that'. It would be the order. Sometimes you'd see them laughing about something. You didn't know whether or not that was a bluff. It wouldn't come out straight away. Maybe a few days, a few weeks. It would never get to us, the collective, at all, until at some point it was necessary that we should know. This was the rule for everything in general, and it was the rule for any information whatsoever about Robbo leaving. Maybe some of the more senior lads had a hint.

When it was time for us to know, we were gathered at The Cliff. We were gutted. Walking into The Cliff, as you walk through the door into the dressing room, my seat was always dead opposite. Denis and Pete sat to the left. Robbo was always at the end on the right, and your line of sight naturally went there as soon as you entered. You'd go in, look right, see Robbo, say hello. That would be it for me. Too scared of saying something stupid. Like I said earlier, he was like a comedian because his delivery of things was absolutely impeccable. The timing of it when it came out was absolutely impeccable. Not always straight away. He could wait. And you'd suffer.

Every time I see Robbo these days it's still the same. I'll make a point of going to a lounge where he's working. And even just sitting there and having a drink with him, I'm still in awe of him. There are few people who I hold in such esteem.

He played his last game for us at Old Trafford against Coventry on the last day of the season. A couple of the kids were playing as some of us were rested. I remember the day well. It was sunny, and I remember all five of the sunny days I experienced in Manchester. Robbo was on 99 league goals for us. Remember what I said about nobody allowing sentiment to get in the way when he needed to score that goal the previous year? Out of the window here – everyone was trying to get him to 100. Maybe too much. But it was his day, his game. It was very emotional for him. The coming days would say a lot about sentiment in football but there's a place for it, of course there is, because Manchester United is such an emotional club. We'd just said goodbye to Sir Matt. And now Robbo was going – the sense of occasion is so great that it naturally impacts the game of football. We drew 0-0. Everyone remembers Bruce and Robbo holding the trophy together again.

The remaining game in the season was the FA Cup Final, where we'd face Chelsea, our bogey side from the league. Life goes on. Football is football. Not even Bryan Robson was safe. The boss named his Wembley team and Robbo wasn't even in the squad. Robbo was different class. He must have been hurting, really, really hurting inside. But I think because of his respect for the boss, his respect for Manchester United as a football club, and obviously us as players, he never showed anything. We were all feeling it as much as him. How can we go into such a historic game and Robbo isn't involved? Once the team was announced, I remember Brucey turning to me and saying about the boss that he's fearless. Absolutely fearless. So there is room for sentiment in football. But if there's history at stake and you feel that your chances are better served with different options, sentiment takes a back seat.

I remember the boss once saying to me, 'Sentiment is a good thing, but it can always get you the sack.' That was the biggest example of that. It doesn't matter who you are. There was never any preparation for it. Never any indication. You couldn't read the situation. He just made the decision and stood by it. If we'd had any indication at all, it's likely that Brucey would have gone and said something. The boss had made a decision that he thought would give him the best chance of ensuring Manchester United would go and win the double.

Everyone wants to play for Manchester United in the FA Cup Final. Nobody could take their place for granted. Eric had a back problem. Brucey had a niggle. Pete was fighting for fitness. I was playing through the pain. Robbo could easily have taken our places (except for Peter) in the squad.

We all wanted our own place in history. We were desperate for it. Winning the league title, and playing so well in retaining it, had earned us plaudits from past heroes. George Best, Denis Law, Bobby Charlton, all of these great man were saying generous things about the way we were playing. You can't be ungrateful but you can't allow yourself to accept those things and, at the time, there's so much going on that it's difficult to take stock of the compliments.

Football's tough, but it's a great king of tough, it's a great job because you're doing what you love. The thing I loved more than anything was getting up and playing football. I didn't want to miss out on any moments, what was going on. And that's what all of us were like. We were like that because of the boss. He found us and brought us to that club because we had that mentality. When someone said they were injured and feeling something, he'd ask the question – can you play? And when they said, no, they were struggling, he knew 100 per cent that they were seriously struggling because they were desperate to play in that game because they knew, or, should

I say, we knew what we were missing in that moment of not playing – all the adulation and everything that went with being in the winning side for Manchester United. We just wanted to be out there.

It was wonderful for legends to say nice things about us but we were desperate to add another episode to the history they'd accomplished. I can tell you that, in those years after I left, I was afflicted by the green-eyed monster, because I wanted to be a part of it when the success continued to roll on. I'd had all that adulation and it was horrible to miss out. But then, after a while, once you realise your time's gone and there's a reason why you're not there anymore and you see it going on, to actually be asked to talk about individuals, to talk about the team, to talk about the manager and what they're going through was absolutely fantastic. A privilege. Likewise, it can be painful when things aren't going well. You can only give a truthful opinion. You want the players to prove you wrong if you criticise them. Understand that next time you see my opinion in the media. You reach a stage in life where your favourite meal is humble pie. You want to take all that and congratulate them while you're eating it. Thanks lads, happy to be doing it. We were lucky in 1994 because things were going well and those who came before were saying nice things. But we had to make our own history to live up to it.

History can be perception. Winning the league title had been historic but it had been done before. That was ending a long hoodoo. But Manchester United had never won the FA Cup and league double. Nobody was talking about that.

It was just… just … an FA Cup Final. We did the cup final record. Had our suits done. Stayed down in London. Arrived at Wembley to see Chelsea players already out on the pitch having their pictures taken. They looked like a Welsh choir in their purple-ish suits. Then it started raining. Their suits went from purple to horribly dark. I had a quick catch-up with Nigel Spackman, now at Stamford Bridge, a former QPR team-mate. He was complaining about the suits they'd been made to wear. Not quite the Liverpool cream suits of 1996 but they hated them all the same.

As I left Nigel, I was accosted by Tom Tyrrell, who interviewed me for the radio.

Tom: 'Any butterflies?'

Me: 'It hasn't really come across yet. I suppose maybe about quarter to three when I'm being presented to the Duchess of Kent it might come to you then. But we'll wait and see really.'

Tom: 'You're getting quite used to playing here this season though. It's United's fourth visit.'

Me: 'You get used to it but still, when it actually starts, it's still the same, and it's still butterflies. I don't think many would say that they'd walk on to Wembley's pitch calm or anything. There's always that little butterfly there somewhere. Some have got bigger ones, some have got smaller ones.'

Tom: 'What's it been like, the build-up this week? Has it been a gradual build-up for you?'

Me: 'No, it's nothing I've actually seen before. It's something completely different. I've been in two League Cup finals and this is ten times bigger than any of them I've seen.

I was involved in the World Cup semi-final but I was away in a foreign country then, so I never actually saw what was going on at home. So this has just been different class really.'

Tom: 'So you've enjoyed it?'

Me: 'Oh yeah, but you don't really enjoy it until you've actually won it, do you? So that makes a difference, doesn't it, really.'

Tom: 'Well, let's see what it's like at quarter to five.'

Me: 'I hope so. Well, that's if you catch me, because you won't be able to catch me if we win it.'

It was massive for me to finally play in a final after watching them for so many years. The closest I'd ever come was a quarter-final with QPR where we narrowly lost to Liverpool at home.

The boss wasn't dismissive of the history associated with the occasion. But his focus was winning the game of football. As far as he was concerned, it was about owing Chelsea something because they made a life a little bit difficult for us in the Premier League because they took six points off of us. He's not normally one for revenge. It's the bigger-picture stuff. Don't get yourself fixated on an opponent. But this was an occasion, so I suppose time to pull that one out. Anything that would give us the edge.

At half-time, though, he'd definitely gone back to Sir Alex Mark 1, because he went absolutely crazy at us after that first-half performance. We were lucky to come in at 0-0. We'd offered little. Gavin Peacock, scorer of the only goal on both occasions Chelsea had beaten us in the league, hit the crossbar. Watch it back now and you can see the rain splash off, it was that torrential. We'd just about got ourselves dry when we had to go back out into it for the second half. I don't know if these things affect you mentally but we were attacking the dressing room end in the second half. We were a bit more at it. Denis did well in one move and Eddie Newton brought him down in the box. Clear penalty. Eric stepped up and, cool as a cucumber, made it 1-0.

A couple of minutes later, Andrei went through. Frank Sinclair brought him down. Chelsea disputed the award of a second penalty – it's possible the rain had made the line of the box difficult to clearly see. Eric was again the calmest man in the stadium. 2-0.

There was a break in play and I was standing next to Tony Cascarino. He looked over at the bench and muttered, 'Here he comes, the superstar. He's going to change the game for us.' There was a sarcastic tone to his voice. I looked and realised Glenn Hoddle, the Chelsea player-manager, was bringing himself on. I shot Tony a look – I was probably just wearing a surprised expression. 'If he does change the game for us, it's going to be a nightmare,' Cas confirmed.

You might have heard the story that the boss was already prepared for this. Brucey tells it quite often. The boss had already seen a situation where Glenn Hoddle puts himself on, and from that point on we'd have control of the game. Perhaps that was on the minds of all the lads. Within a minute of him stripping off and coming on to the pitch, Sparky had been put through and made it 3-0. Right at the end, Choccy – on the bench at the expense of Robbo – showed the great team spirit at the club by setting up Ince to score into an empty net when he could easily have scored himself.

Was it a fantastic second-half performance? No, but we went from being awful to being half-decent, and did what was necessary. We played the game, not the occasion, and made our own history in the process.

The FA Cup Final was our 63rd match of the season. For most of the season, the boss had relied on 14 players. Just 14 players who played more than ten matches, though I'd always say the squad was 16 of us (Dion made ten appearances, and Mick Phelan made eight). It was a phenomenal effort and you could say the end of the season came at the right time. Four European Cup games, getting to a League Cup Final when two rounds were two legs and one went to a replay, winning the FA Cup with a semi-final replay, and playing 42 matches in the league. Winning the double. Incredible.

I talked about winning trophies being done in Brucey's living room. Here, we all had the luxury of playing for 20 minutes knowing we were going to make history. It was some kind of fantasy. An out-of-body experience because you can afford yourself a moment when you go, so this is the FA Cup Final. This is what I watched on telly all those years. In a bit I'm going to be wearing a silly hat and a scarf. Then I thought to myself, no, my memory is that every FA Cup Final is sunny. That's the law, isn't it? Why did I have to get the one where it pisses it down the full day? But then the whistle goes, you get your medal in your hand, you get to hold the cup, it's a matter of seconds and minutes where the dream you've had for your entire life comes true. You won the FA Cup playing for Manchester United. This isn't your back garden kickaround. This is that dream fulfilled. And we'd done it, deservedly so. We were worthy of it.

There didn't need to be any conceit or arrogance associated with that. Just a pride and a sense of accomplishment. It was a season where we'd played some of our best football, and much of it was played in the FA Cup. In the third round we'd scored a goal at Sheffield United where almost all of us had a touch in the build-up. We'd done what we did at Wimbledon. I knew then that nobody would ever forget Sparky's goal against Oldham – and nobody has. In that moment it was worth the sacrifice of the pain and discomfort I was still feeling in my ankle.

We did the post-match interviews. I let everybody know on television that I was going to have a beer. That clip's done the rounds on social media. It wasn't so much the celebrations but the morning after, waking up having finished the season with three medals – two as winners and one as a runner-up. It's difficult to properly explain the context to a modern fan or younger reader, because I run the risk of trying to embellish the size of the achievement for the sake of my own ego. But in over 100 years, only five teams had ever won the league and FA Cup double, and it had only been done three times in the 20th century – by Spurs in 1961, Arsenal in 1971 and Liverpool in 1986. As I write this in 2025, it's already been won four times in the 21st century.

So the scale of the achievement spoke for itself. Football was different in 1994 to how it was in 1964, and it evolved again in 2024. Players are more athletic, the balls are lighter. The ball was in play for longer periods than it is now, tackles were more aggressive, games were allowed to run. And, of course, in the modern age, what counts as competition has completely changed, dictated by the resources of Manchester City. At United in 1994 we were just starting to emerge as the dominant team, and not because we had the greatest resources, paid the biggest fees or had the biggest squad. Of course, going back, Liverpool in the 80s would say the same about their own dominant period, and how it was a golden time for English football with Nottingham Forest and Aston Villa both having won European Cups. Maybe every player thinks theirs was the golden generation; I just know I wouldn't swap the era I played in. There was the perfect balance of everything healthy in the game before money became king.

There was also the perfect balance of respect. Players respecting their managers, and managers respecting their players. That could be seen by what happened with Robbo. The boss had his vindication for his decision. We'd won the cup, comfortably. We'd made history. Before the game, after the game, you never knew any different as far as Robbo was concerned. You'd think that he'd led us out, he'd lifted the trophy, he'd played the same role as he had in his prior three performances for United in FA Cup finals. As far as he was concerned, we won it together.

The boss had two modes of congratulating you. Every game was a big game. You'd come through the changing room doors, and he'd give you a slap around the back of the head, if he'd had to give you a rollicking on the pitch, saying, 'I told you that you could do it.' It was a bit different with the finals. He and Kiddo would grab a drink. To a certain extent he'd almost become one of the lads. If you'd given everything for him, he'd become one of us. You knew, all of us knew, how far to go. Certain players would go further, because they'd earned the right to. But before long he'd remind you about the following year. And he'd never let that go, he'd always remind you, 'If you've got anything about you, you'd want to do this again.' You could still be in the moment and he was of the presence to remind you that you need to have it again. It was always about doing it again. Once was never enough.

15

Breaking Down

I WAS feeling okay during pre-season. It's only with hindsight that I can describe the issues with my ankle as a gamble, because I actually didn't see it that way at the time. I felt I'd come through the worst of it. I'd made a decision not to rest it during the run-in and I didn't regret that – I'd been involved in historic occasions that, as you can tell, meant something significant to me, and I'd never forget it, or trade it. I'm incredibly proud of the fact that people include my name when they speak about the 1992 to 1994 team.

Just as we started to get ready for the new league season, I felt a twinge in the ankle again. I was honest with the boss but didn't want to play it up. He asked if I felt it would be alright, because I was important to his plans – the format of the Champions League had changed, and we now had six guaranteed group games. I could have said no, my ankle is going to come first. Truthfully, I didn't take it as seriously as I should have done. My thought was that an operation may fix it, but it might not even be necessary. It might just go away in time. It would sort itself out. What did I know?

I had no medical training, no certificates to show that I was some kind of doctor. The question I was asking myself at my core was: did I think I'd be able to get through it? Would I get through and be a 100 per cent? I believed I would. I said I was okay.

The manager never once stressed to me that I was needed because of my nationality, what with the foreigner rule still imposed by UEFA. It was more about my own importance. People talk about the following year as one where big outgoing transfers happened but there were a few in 1994, too. Lee Martin had already gone, meaning Denis would always have to play left-back (and Lee Sharpe would have to cover for him). Mick Phelan, who could cover on the right, also left. And Clayton Blackmore, who could play both sides, followed Robbo to Middlesbrough, where he'd become player-manager. The boss had signed David May from Blackburn. There was also a junior player by the name of Gary Neville who was ready to make regular appearances.

If there was a competitive fight, I was ready for it mentally, but circumstances prevented that from ever really happening, because once the season started I couldn't get any momentum going. On the opening day of the season I was sent off. The rules had changed over the summer following the World Cup, and referees were now instructed to send off players for tackles from behind. Les Ferdinand was a big bloke. Far too big a bloke to go down as easily as he did under my challenge. I told him that as well. But I was sent off, against my old team QPR of all teams, and ended up with a three-game suspension, which was bad enough but especially when we'd just signed a new player. So Maysie was given a fair run at right-back.

I was told to keep myself fresh, as I was needed for Europe. It wasn't easy to do, fitness-wise – I was one of those people who needed games. I needed to play games to keep me at a sharp edge all the time. It was difficult to jump in and out of games, especially of the magnitude they are for Manchester United. It's a very, very difficult thing to do, and requires a certain personality. I started to think about the injury. It weighed on my mind. What was I all about? My strengths were turning quickly on a sixpence, my mobility, the fact I couldn't be caught out. I dwelled on the fact that all of my dynamism seemed to depend on the axis of my ankle. I knew my mobility had been impacted. There were so many times when I knew I should have been half a yard tighter. I was telling myself I can't go there, because if the ball was to go in behind me, I didn't believe in my head that I was going to be able to recover, because I was always going to be worried about twisting on that ankle.

The boss was, as always, as good as his word. I came off the bench in our return to Galatasaray – a repeat of our 0-0 draw seemed like a decent result considering it came so early in the group. A couple of weeks later we played Sheffield Wednesday and I was back in. I wasn't right. It was more mental hindrance, if I'm being brutally honest with myself, because a lot of the pain was equalised by the tablets and cortisone. I didn't realise the damage I was doing to my body. My love for the game and my desperation to be part of everything that was happening at the club was all that mattered to me. I didn't want to miss it. Now, if you were to say to me at that point in time in the autumn of 1994 that this is how it's going to end, this is what you're going to endure, I'd have said, please get me off the ride and let me get the ankle sorted properly. It's a strange environment to be in at Old Trafford. It's an alluring, addictive thing. And when you're there but not in it, it can be difficult. I was 30, at my peak. You don't get much longer – your career ends in your 30s. You want to play as often as possible. You want to win.

I wanted the occasions, just like my next game, against Barcelona at Old Trafford. We went a goal up early on through Sparky. The roof came off. It was unbelievable. Fifteen minutes later, Romário, their Brazilian superstar, equalised. I'd been selected to play in the middle because of my man-marking ability. Romário was my man. They had a corner and Pally had said to me, 'Parks, I've got him.' That was part and parcel of what was bred into footballers during that era. You took responsibility upon yourself. As much as the game plan was for me to do it, Pally took responsibility. From a passage of open play, a ball was slipped through. Romário ran across me, across Pally. I couldn't adjust quickly enough. Pally said, 'He's mine,' or words to that effect. He took the job off me but Romário was just too quick, and nipped in to score.

The manager lost his head at half-time. It was 1-1. I answered back – what could I do? I wasn't going to argue about it, though. The boss was right. I'd been told to do something. Sometimes you have to take responsibility and be willing to accept the consequences at the end of it. That was it. Nine times out of ten, that comes off, and when you talk about it with your manager, they actually maybe want to pat you on the back or something, just for having the foresight and the bravery to take it on. It's a story that has been told by all three of us. The boss was right. Maybe something that gets lost in the story is that Romário was one of the greatest strikers of all time. He was absolutely lethal. People talk about Ronaldo and Ronaldinho, about the modern greats. Romário rarely gets a mention but he had an incredible box of tricks. For someone of his body shape, such a low knee lift as well, his first three or four yards were so quick – rather than just a run, it was almost a fast waddle. He was one of those players who could send you to sleep in the game, because he just jogged and jogged, then once he'd gone, he'd gone. It was as simple as that. The boss read the riot act to me and Pally at half-time. In the second half, a great game was concluded by an extravagant Sharpey goal to get us a 2-2 draw.

Barcelona also had Stoichkov. They had a great side, in fairness, and Stoichkov was another who'd been brilliant at the World Cup. He was technically unbelievable as well, especially at the Camp Nou in the infamous return game. I've seen Stoichkov twice since that game, in old-boy matches, and every time he goes, 'Parker, Parker! Four nil!' with that big smile on his face as well. He's a funny man. The Camp Nou match was horrendous. That was the best of that Barcelona team. The manager could have all the tactical plans he wanted but the thing out of his control was the foreigner rule, and while I wouldn't go so far as to definitively say we'd have won this or that if that rule wasn't in place, it was obvious that it impacted us in some games more than others. For that match, we were already missing Eric, who was still suspended from the previous season's episode with Galatasaray, and the boss decided to play Gary Walsh instead of Schmeichel. We were going from a team that could win games of football on a Saturday to changing the entire dynamic of that side for European competition. Continuity was key to the boss, and one of the things he championed most was the idea of good performances before big games. It was impossible to generate that sort of consistency of performance when he was restricted with the continuity of his selection.

That didn't get us off the hook. Barcelona in that mood would have done that to anybody but it was against a depleted Manchester United team who were still getting the hairdryer. He's going at a few people, finally gets to me. 'And you,' he says, 'you can just fucking go and get your ankle sorted.' Within 48 hours I was in Princess Grace Hospital having my ankle operation.

They say mud sticks, and my two thoughts were: I'd not played often and my last performance had come in a 4-0 defeat. The last thing I wanted was for that to be the thing that people were thinking about. He wasn't fit, he's finished, that sort of thing. Remember that Barcelona 4-0? That was the end of him.

I did have a certain sense of relief. There was that feeling that the decision had been taken out of my hands, the operation was coming and everything would be fine. I was going to be me again, Paul Parker. I had the operation, felt pretty good afterwards. The doctor came in and goes, 'Yeah, it went well. You'll be alright playing football. But, just know, it's never going to be the same as it was before. Too much ligament damage. You'll do well to get back to where you were.'

I think if he'd said that to me today, or even if I was 20 and not 30, I'd have probably had the bug of wanting to prove them wrong. But I'd spent a lot of time being worn down by it. I didn't feel like myself. I didn't feel as though the fight would do any good. So, because I was at such a low ebb, that natural fight I had, the fight that had pushed back against whatever had been said to me, never came in to it. I shrank. Those words stayed with me. *It's never going to be the same.*

We were eliminated from the Champions League at the group stage. No, like I said, you won't find me declaring with certainty that we'd have won the competition without the foreigner rule. But when people criticise the boss and say he should have won more in Europe, they should look at how the competition changed in the 90s, how it evolved after the turn of the century, and compare the strength of the competition to how weak it is now.

Everything at the club was impacted. For instance, the manager's response to elimination was to go into the transfer market and sign a striker. He had to sign an English one. Two names were mentioned – Stan Collymore and Andy Cole. Collymore was a good striker but I think the boss made the right choice. Coley was sensational. He was quick, dangerous around the box, a brilliant finisher. He was already great but when he came to Old Trafford he improved so much. At Newcastle he was always facing the goal. At United he learned to play with his back to goal. Now, was he taught to do that? I don't know, but I think about how he was and how he conducted himself, and I'd say he personally felt it was important to do that, in the way that Manchester United play, so that he could be that person always available to people to play off. He learned to do that but he never lost the instinct to score goals.

Coley learned to play on his own as well. He didn't always have someone next to him to link to but he learned to do that too. A short time with Eric, Teddy Sheringham and Dwight Yorke, most obviously. He went from being a very good striker to one of the best centre-forwards in the country. One of the best we've *ever* had. He's also, however, one of the most unlucky players as well, because for some reason no one wants to talk to or about Andy Cole. Maybe it's his honesty. No grey era with him, and maybe that's gone against him in a sense in that way … but you speak to any players of that era and nobody devalues Andy. So it's amazing how he gets bypassed. Today the football shows talk about forwards, they show the stats, put a graph up, you'll see Andy Cole sitting above almost anyone they care to name. He knows it, Coley, and it bothers him. It would bother anybody. But it doesn't come across in his demeanour. He's class and elegance. He always looked elegant when he scored poacher's goals. He also scored outstanding goals from outside the box. I can't speak highly enough of him. It took him a little while to settle in at the club, and it didn't help that he signed and then we had one of the most turbulent moments in our history the following week.

I was sitting on the bench at Selhurst Park as we went down there to play Palace. It was 0-0 at half-time. Richard Shaw, their defender, had been having a running battle with Eric. Eric had one of those moments again and was sent off. He was walking off the side of the pitch to the tunnel then somebody ran down to the front of the stand to have a go at him. Apparently the lad was running down to the toilet, something like that. There was the conflict that everybody now is aware of, the images anybody reading this immediately brings to mind. It was amazing. You think you'll never see anything like that again. If that happened today, would that player be treated as harshly as Eric was? I don't think so.

There was the comical moment after the match that everybody now knows. The boss had a go at everyone because we only drew 1-1. Got to Eric and said, 'You can't be doing that, son.'

They went all-in on Eric big time from the outside. The club tried to act fast by suspending him for the rest of the season but the FA just had to make it worse. It was much too harsh. It was like someone had said, let's take a little bit of sting out the tail of Manchester United. Take away one of their key elements, maybe the biggest element in Eric Cantona, and make it as hard as possible for them to retain the league.

Eric was suspended but he was always around. He faced criminal charges and got community service, which was to work with a load of kids. Busloads came in. The easiest thing to do, maybe nine out of ten people would do, would be just show up, be there and leave it to the community coaches United had. But Eric took part, joined in, and those kids absolutely loved it. Eric was spotless in everything he did with regards his reaction to the punishment, even when you might have thought he could easily have just phoned it in.

His absence cost us, we can't say anything other than that. He wasn't the only one missing. Andrei had a hernia and fell out with the boss. Ryan had a hamstring issue. We did well to get through the season and still, on the last day, be in with a chance of winning both the league and the FA Cup. We deserved a pat on the back for being so competitive but the tone of the press was so negative.

The league was so competitive. Blackburn had spent big again and were now on the verge of stopping us getting to three in a row. You didn't go to a game and expect the champions to play anyone and beat them heavily, in the same way you have with Manchester City almost every week for the last few years. That's a comment on the competitive value of the league. They won four in a row at a canter. Everybody was trying to stop us. Kicking us off the park, spending more money, and even the FA had their little go.

It was agony watching it. And I don't just mean watching us draw at West Ham while Blackburn lost at Anfield and still won the league. I don't just mean losing the FA Cup Final. I'm talking about complete FOMO, I was in a horrible place mentally. When we scored and won, could I celebrate? No, because I wanted to be a part of it, and I was too close to it. I hated when we lost and I couldn't help. I hated the sensation of not feeling like I was getting any closer to a return. I should have done more. I don't think I was putting myself in the best possible position of coming back, of winning my place in the team deservedly. I just had those words of the doctor in my mind and I'd almost accepted them as some form of inevitable defeat, no matter what I did.

Change happens and you just begin to accept you're part of it. We lost a lot of senior experience when most people were expecting us to strengthen to compete with Blackburn. Andrei Kanchelskis had fallen out with the manager and nobody really knew what had happened. There were rumours about bungs and the mafia and I didn't know anything about that, all I know is I thought it was incredibly strange that a player of such talent left Manchester United to sign for Everton at that particular time. Everton are traditionally a great football club, an old English football club, and Goodison Park was always a great traditional place to go in football, but it just didn't strike me as the sort of move a player like Andrei would make. Through his broken English and my non-existent Russian, we struck up a relationship that just wouldn't exist without my life taking me to Manchester United. I adored him as a player and as a person. He was a funny man, and whenever I've bumped into him after our retirement we've always shared a laugh.

So it didn't really make much sense to me, especially considering Incey went to Inter Milan, and that was the sort of profile we're talking about with Andrei too. If I ask you what was the best in-house battle at Old Trafford from 1993 to 1995, you might react instinctively and say Ince vs the boss. No. It was Incey against Roy Keane. Incey was always going to be better than Roy, he had to be, he believed he was. His game went up another level when Roy turned up, because he wanted to run further, he wanted to make more tackles, win more balls, score more goals. It was almost like he knew Keano had been earmarked as the next Robson and he was keen to show he could do that job. It was an incredible internal rivalry, which transformed us on the pitch. They bit at each other off the pitch, little witty remarks to each other. Never snide, always competitive.

Paul's ego often earned him moments of conflict with the boss. Incey was popular but divisive. He was a great player for Manchester United and he was great at West Ham. He was playing there at a time when being a black player was tough, and he got away with being a black player at West Ham because he was good. He was so focused and he'd make everything about him. You couldn't say another midfielder was good. *I'm better than him.* That's how he was. *I'm better than him.* He'd want to go out and prove it, and he usually did.

In my first season we played at Luton and I was jockeying Mick Harford on the halfway line. Incey came in and savaged him. I was being careful – didn't want to upset someone like Mick. Ince piled in with his trademark slide-tackle. Dominated him. Got up, pulled up his shorts, those tight little Adidas shorts, as he was running away. Yeah, Paul was a big character. But ask anyone who played with him at Old Trafford and most of them will say they loved him. Paul played in the same team as my brother when he was a kid, so I'd known of him for a long time. He was extremely competitive, desperate to win. He had a proper tough upbringing. It impacted the way he conducted himself and how he chose to respect and trust people. He had that sensibility about him – I won't ask anybody to do it, I'll do it myself because I know I can do it. He brought that into football and that's what made him a great player for Manchester United. It's also possibly that big character that made conflict with the boss inevitable.

He started coming in to the club saying Inter Milan were in for him. The boss had got wind of that. I think he realised that sort of thing wouldn't be said if Incey hadn't admitted to them he was interested. So when the offer came in, the manager probably knew it had been invited, and called Incey's bluff. Accepted the offer. Go on then, you can go. Paul then tried to say he didn't want to go. And you know what – he probably didn't. He's an East London boy like me. Made Manchester his second home. But he made the boss think, and the boss thought, I've got Keane, Nicky Butt breaking through, Paul Scholes too. Made the boss's mind up for him. And the boss could say you've brought this on yourself. Made your bed. Lie in it.

I don't think Paul found it easy in Italy. The speed of his return to England proved that. But he made friends over there and I think made the most of it. It made a big difference to his life and I think it improved him as a player on a technical level.

The other famous departure that summer was Mark Hughes. Lovely man, unless you're against him on the football pitch. Someone who seemed to represent everything the club stood for. He'd been away and come back. You couldn't imagine the place without him. But he went, and I think Sparky more than the other two made me realise that this was going to be a very different United moving forward. I couldn't help but think of the words of Steve Bruce a year earlier. This boss is fearless. It was brutal. And you knew he was making those decisions to improve the team because that was all that mattered to him.

Of course, not everybody shared his conviction. On the opening day of the following season we lost 3-1 at Villa Park. I was back in the team for my first senior game since Barcelona. I felt ready to play again. My performances suggested otherwise, and probably contributed to the manager thinking I'd had my time. I wasn't ready, my body wasn't prepared, and I'll accept that it probably contributed to a memorable defeat. Villa Park had always been one of my favourite places to play. Not that day. We lost 3-1, and had a bunch of young lads in the side.

That night on *Match of the Day*, Alan Hansen uttered his immortal line: 'You can't win anything with kids.' Time would prove him wrong but I think *more* time has helped put his comment in perspective. When he said it, at the time a lot of fans would have thought that as well. Many people felt the boss had gone one step too far here.

Who are they, who are we, to question a man who'd earned the right to make such a bold decision? He had every right to go and try those things. He saved the club a lot of money. He and Eric Harrison already knew what they'd worked with and knew what they were going to grow into. What's a return on investment measured in? Money, usually. For Manchester United and Alex Ferguson, it was trophies that mattered most. I don't know how you could put a value on the wisdom of his foresight in 1995.

16

The Hard Goodbye

I PLAYED a handful of games in my final season at Old Trafford. When you're playing for Manchester United, you want everything to have a cherry on top, but it doesn't always work out like that, and it didn't for me.

What's true is that most of those appearances were memorable or infamous for one reason or another. I wouldn't have chosen Rotor Volgograd away as my last European appearance for the most famous club in the world. I came off the bench for Scholes as the boss settled for a goalless draw. I think I'd have preferred to have stayed wrapped up with the blankets.

I think I'd become a little consumed by the amount of change. My mindset wasn't right, I was thinking about my fitness, I had that physical wall that stops you doing the natural thing, because subconsciously I knew my ankle wasn't up to it. Even Old Trafford was different, there was a big redevelopment of the North Stand and you couldn't help but feel that there was this moment of transition and, with the struggles I had, I'd already accepted that I wouldn't survive it as a United player.

We played Bolton at Old Trafford. No Andrei in front of me – a little skinny lad called Terry Cooke. But he was sprightly and had that bit of energy in front of me and, given everything that I'd gone through, it made a positive difference. It helped my game to have someone like him who was enthusiastic, wanted to make a point … he couldn't help himself, he was tracking back, was covering, was doing everything really. It was a decent day, and a bit of an occasion because Terry was joined by a few of the younger lads and we went on to win 3-0. It was good to be involved in that. Terry was made more for the modern game. I don't know whether there was enough meat on the bone for him at that time, but with his natural dribbling ability and the changes in the way you can tackle, he'd have been a fans' favourite today because of his honesty, his passion, the way he played with a smile on his face, his resilience, the little bit of bite in his game. I know he ended up in America in the end. He was a nice lad.

It was another youthful side that went out against York City at Old Trafford but still enough experience to not be writing about an embarrassing 3-0 defeat. I don't know if that or the 4-1 home defeat to my old club QPR was more embarrassing. Paul Barnes, whose son Harvey now plays for Newcastle, scored twice. He won a bike for winning man of the match. So the knives came out and people were questioning the kids again, but at the end of the day I was involved and I still look at that game and I can certainly not blame anyone around. I'm looking at myself and I question my performance. I have to, because we got embarrassed at home. It's one I'd prefer to forget.

If it was possible, I was even more embarrassed with myself the following weekend, even though we got a respectable 0-0 draw at Sheffield Wednesday. Terry, Scholesy, Becks and Simon Davies were all playing, as was Nicky Butt, my old boot boy. Nicky played me a pass. It was a decent pass. I couldn't get there. My first thought, shamefully, was to give Nicky the glare. You know the one – the one that an experienced player gives a kid. You should have done better. It hurt me then and it hurts now. It was the typical old pro thing, the thing I swore I'd never do. Put the blame on someone else. Pretend it's not me. Sorry, Nicky. That's when I really knew that I was struggling. I've had a go at players for doing that very thing. I wasn't brave enough to admit the truth, but there was no hiding from it for me. I knew I couldn't carry on, as I was doing myself no justice.

Almost mercifully, I was out of the side then for a bit. I was then back in thanks to an injury crisis over Christmas. We lost at Leeds on Christmas Eve. I was poor, static, scared of pushing through on the ankle. In the next game the boss chose Keano at right-back. That was tough. That's the manager saying, you're just not good enough. You're not being good enough. You don't deserve to play. Then you go back in time, and you think about all the good times, and with my contract expiring at the end of the season, I knew my time was up. It didn't help that Roy was brilliant, and scored in a crucial 2-0 win over Newcastle.

You want to go and ask the boss questions, without a shadow of a doubt. Players do go and ask questions. I told myself I didn't have to go and ask because I knew the answer. I knew my time was going to be up. I'd geared myself towards it, even though I still had an involvement. I was still around everybody, still doing everything regarding what Manchester United were doing as a team. I was still with the lads, mates with all the lads, but I knew it was coming to the end. But every now and again, there were moments where I geared myself up to say, well, this time next year, I won't be here. I won't be in Manchester. That's what it became like in the end. And in a way, I kind of talked myself out of it, mentally talked myself out of Manchester United. I don't think there was enough gas in the tank, you know, for me to drive through it and prove a point.

I wish that I *had* gone and seen the boss a lot earlier and spoken to him about what I was feeling, because I think his approach would have been different to how it was at the end. I think at the end of it, he saw seen me as somebody who he didn't need and want anymore, because he was seeing that I'd thrown the towel in and accepted it, which wasn't me, because I never got to Manchester United being that way. But I changed, something changed within me to just accept that my time was up.

I didn't know it at the time but my last Old Trafford game for the first team came against QPR. Thankfully it was won 2-1. Most people remember that for the debut of William Prunier, a mate of Eric's, who came in on trial. I think if Eric had brought his cousin, his mum or anybody and told the boss that they'd do a good job, the boss would have given them a go. But he brought William along and he was a lovely fella, and he just had a decent game. It was the set-up for a bad punchline, as that trial concluded with a disastrous game at Spurs. Chris Armstrong had his best-ever game, scoring twice, as we lost 4-1. The boss was livid. Hated losing to London sides. It was no better for me, having grown up a Spurs fan, to now suffer what was their equivalent of winning the treble. I might have chosen White Hart Lane as the venue for my last United league game if I couldn't have Old Trafford, but not in those circumstances.

My last two games came in the FA Cup. I started at Sunderland but was off the pitch when Coley scored in the last minute to send us through. He'd had a lot of stick after missing some chances on the last day of the league season at West Ham, and had suffered some injuries, but had started to show signs of his real form. That win earned us a fourth-round clash at Reading.

That tie at Elm Park should have been called off because the pitch was iced over and almost impossible to play on. When I played for Fulham, I lived in Wokingham, so I was known in the area. I was a sub, so warming up and coming on I got a healthy dose of booing. I came on and got straight into the game. The ball was given to me – my first touch, boos raining in – and I moved forward with the ball. Eric and Sharpey both made runs. I wanted to whip the ball in so it was a good area for either of them behind the defence.

The ball bobbled up on the awful pitch and my connection with it came almost right on the top of my foot. The Reading goalkeeper was Nicky Hammond. He was a year or two younger than me. He went to school with my brother in senior school. So, I've known Nicky since he was a young kid. He must have seen what I was doing because he moved to his right, thinking I was going to look to whip it. However, it hit the front of my foot, and the ball just whipped the other way and went in at the near post to his left. Now, if I had any experience of scoring, that could have been given goal of the month or something, but I think I gave the game away with my surprised celebration. It settled us down, because it gave us a 2-0 lead, and we eventually won 3-0.

I suppose if you were going to say you wanted the cherry on the cake, then scoring in your last game for Manchester United is a good way to go out. But it was January. There was a long time to go until the end of the season. I won't have been the only one to have spent their last few months in the first-team wilderness. I don't know whether they call them strong-willed or stupid, because there's nothing worse than being around somewhere and not playing. It's not a good feeling. It wasn't a good feeling.

But I balance that with what I did experience. I played in the reserve side. While the first team were hunting Newcastle down for the Premier League title, my last game at any level for the club came in a 2-0 reserve-team win against Newcastle. We won the reserve-team league. I got a tankard for winning.

When I was a kid playing reserve-team football for Fulham, I remember those 2pm kick-offs and the teams with the old pros who were quite bitter and wondering what they were doing there. So they'd be leaving the game maybe about 5pm and it would take them ages to get home. An entire Saturday lost and they weren't even in the first team. There were a few shouts and screams and angry challenges and I can remember looking at them, hoping I never turned into one of them.

You could say it was different because there was a generational buzz going on at United. I'd played the odd reserve game over the years. One I think was at Chesterfield against Derby. They had to delay the kick-off because so many people were trying to get in. They were desperate to see the new generation of United kids everyone was raving about. When you're playing alongside that, any danger of having an attitude quickly gets wiped away because you see what the young kids are giving and what they can do. My whole thing when I played with them was not to mug myself off. I had to show what I was and that meant I had to work hard, I had to concentrate to make sure that I didn't do anything to let those lads down by just trying to drift through a game and act like I was a senior pro. I could have done whatever I wanted and none of them would have called me out. Just like Nicky didn't in Sheffield. They'd accept what I was as a senior pro and they'd have kind of shrugged their shoulders and got on with it. But I wasn't going to let myself down. I certainly wasn't going to let those kids down and I wasn't going to mug myself off in front of Jimmy Ryan, who was the reserve-team manager. I wasn't going to allow him to go back and say things about me in that way to the boss, which Jimmy would have had a right to do – but I never gave him that opportunity, because it wasn't me.

And, to be perfectly honest, I loved it. I absolutely loved playing with those kids. The atmosphere of those games as well was incredible, because everybody was getting through those turnstiles to watch these kids. That's what it boiled down to. They were really, really good occasions to play in those games. I played and I was captain and I won a league title. It was really good and in a way that did brighten it at the end, that bit of involvement with those kids. It should be impossible for anyone to let themselves down. You could have a bad game, but to go on to a pitch with a bad attitude would have been one of the biggest crimes ever.

From time to time those young lads who developed into legends of the club do give me the honour of mentioning my name, usually favourably. There's a great deal of satisfaction that comes from that. Despite what those lads went and did, and what they're doing now, they still remember that time – it's nice. If they're not talking about you, if they don't mention you, there's a reason why.

United won the league and FA Cup double in 1996. By today's qualification standards, given I played a few games for the first team and played in the cup, I'd qualify for a winner's medal, but the criteria at the time meant I didn't. It's been suggested to me that the question could be asked. Am I a three-time league title winner? Am I included in the side that won the double double? I can't say that I feel that, and even if I was to get a winner's medal, if I put it together with what I'd already won, it wouldn't mean anything different to me. I don't think people would have a different perception. There's the odd time when I do think, *Yeah, maybe I should have three title medals*. But I can't say it with any conviction. I can't say I truly deserve it.

The criteria at the time was something like ten games and I didn't play ten games … if it was a third of a season, maybe. Look, I'm talking about this because of what United won in 1996, not because I feel any entitlement. Quite the opposite. I feel like I'm just very, very lucky that I won what I won with Manchester United. I didn't have a manager trying to do me a favour or get me on the pitch all the time so I could earn a medal. I was wanted and needed out there to play. I've got the medals and I've got the scars and everything else, what my body's been through, to prove it.

The Tuesday after the FA Cup Final I plucked up the courage to see the boss and really get it over and done with. I knew my time was up, there were no doubts about that. I hadn't done anywhere near good enough. I'd known that for months but on the actual day and at the meeting I was churning up inside because, as much as you might think you can prepare yourself for it, there's nothing like leaving United. I also had no idea of what would come next after leaving. I tried my best to not show the manager how I was feeling. Tried to deal with it like a man, like the professional he knew.

You might read this and think I'm being harsh on myself. That a lot of it was down to an injury. It was, but I still knew I hadn't personally done enough. I knew that I hadn't given myself the best chance, and that's the bit I hold against myself.

Many years later I had my hip replaced and a ceramic one put in its place. I had the replacement because of my ankle injury. I'd been compensating all those years with my body shape, all the games I played, all the anti-inflammatories I took, and it eventually took a toll on my hip. I had dedicated rehabilitation with a woman who owned a gym. She was an ex-nurse and she gave me this routine. I was going early in the morning with her, from half-past six, and then from half-past seven, I was doing my own bit, and I was doing it every day for a month. Then someone talked to me about the way I was walking and I almost had to learn again. I had some tests done to see where the distortion was and there were special exercises to do over a six-month period. I did my own physio and rehab through that and was determined to make it through because I never wanted to have another operation like that or leave something until it was at such a stage that it was impossible or pointless to have one. I mention this because that's the old me. I had the fire in me to do that. And I just wish I'd been that way in late 1994 and not just allowed myself to be beaten by a doctor's words when I was better than that, especially considering everything else I'd already overcome in order to make it to where I had. It was so minor in the bigger picture.

The boss was good about it. He spoke about Gary's emergence at right-back. He said, 'Paul, I'd love to keep you, but we need to move on. I could be sentimental, but I can't, because sentiment could cost me my job.'

It was an incredible sentence, really. One I've remembered and one I've used myself many times. One I'm grateful for now.

But I wasn't at the time. I didn't take it that way. Everything I'd bottled up for nearly a year came out in anger. Not at the boss, just the situation. The idea of leaving United. I'd left clubs I loved before. I had great years at Fulham. Even greater years with QPR. But Manchester United was more than football. It was a family. It had become my life, something I was defined by. Who was I without it? I'm not sure I was ready to find out.

Time did the thing time does, and it got easier. I never fell out with the boss. When I think about what he said, it was one of the nicest things he could have said. He goes further than that. Whenever he'd talk about his great defenders, my name would get added to the list. Having the stamp of approval from the boss is an incredible thing. If I'd fallen out with him in any way and left on bad terms, my connection with Manchester would have been very, very difficult. I wouldn't feel justified, I couldn't feel comfortable walking around.

Every time I go to a game when he's there, I always make sure I see him. One recent time I was up for a game, maybe in 2023, and, I was with Robbo and Pally. I went off to look for Denis in the lounge where he was working. As I cut through, I passed the directors' area, so I thought I'd better pop in and see if the boss was in. I went up and said hello.

'I always make sure I come and see you, boss,' I said.

'Well,' he goes, 'I knew you were in here three-quarters of an hour ago. The game's about to kick-off. I was wondering whether or not you were going to come and see me!'

Somehow he still knows everything that's going on. I don't think he needed to ask the window cleaner for that one.

17

Falling Out of and Back in Love with the Game

LOOK THROUGH my Wikipedia, read any description of my career and one team is usually missing. With good reason, as I never played for them, but it was still a team that played a big role in the direction of my career.

Derby County made an offer for me. They'd just been promoted into the Premier League, were managed by Jim Smith, my old boss. They presented me with a two-year deal, when I was informed that Marseille had enquired about my availability and fitness. They wanted to take me on trial for a week to prove my fitness and then they'd offer me a deal. At the time, Marseille were the biggest club in France, and that was a boost to my ego after leaving United, so I accepted the trial even though the pride took a bit of a jab with the 'having to prove myself' part. But I went, and went with the right attitude, proved myself, proved to myself that my ankle was okay. The coach, Gérard Gili, said he wanted to sign me. He laid out his plan. I'd be played at right-back in home games, and in away games he played three at the back, so I was going to play as a man-marker. The negotiations were handled by Eric's brother, Joël, who had connections there. That was helpful to me as my French was poor. I was shown around the stadium, told about the developments in place for the World Cup in a couple of years, and Joël said everything was sorted. There was a good feeling, a good vibe.

In the cab on the way back to the airport, my agent called me. 'I'm not sure this is gonna happen, Paul.' I thought that was strange. When I finally got home to Manchester, I had a call from Joël, who told me it had fallen through. I asked why. He didn't say. I had a chat with the boss. He said my agent had asked for some money up front, the club had refused and killed the deal there and then. If I'd known his plan, I'd have given him a bit more from what I was getting – it was a good deal and a good move for me. I was gutted. Obviously, I ended my partnership with my agent. Didn't talk to him, for obvious reasons.

I went back cap-in-hand to Jim and Derby. That two-year offer had turned into a three-month trial. Jim was great, there were good lads in the squad and the club seemed in a good place, but I felt uncomfortable from the moment that offer changed, even though I understood it. My impression was that there were people dealing with the money side of things who weren't really happy. I was already prepared for this discomfort when I discovered that a few players weren't happy with Jim's assistant, Steve McClaren. They didn't trust him, so one of the lads made up some nonsense story, I can't even remember what it was, but something to see whether Steve was going back to the boss with everything. So, within an hour of this story being mentioned on the training ground, Jim came out and called us all together to have a go at us. 'We can't even talk on the training ground,' one of the lads complained. I didn't feel right. Didn't really do myself justice either.

Nigel Spackman got in touch. He was working as a coach with Howard Kendall at Sheffield United and asked if I wanted to have a trial there. Sheffield United were quite a vibrant club, they'd been in the Premier League and had ambitions of returning. They had a few good pros there like Don Hutchinson, Gareth Taylor and David Holdsworth. Dane Whitehouse was the local prospect and someone I got on very well with. Every club has their prospect, don't they? Someone who could have made it big. Well, Dane could have been a great player, but he'd suffered a knee injury. I enjoyed my very brief time at Bramall Lane but I knew it wasn't working out, because I still hadn't got Manchester United out of my system. Howard was decent about it, we both knew it wasn't right, so over Christmas I left and was without a club again.

I had offers to go to Australia and America. The Australian one was more serious – there was a local club in Joondalup and they were associated with Perth Glory. I'd play one part of the season for both sides. I was thinking about it, probably thinking more on the side of refusing it really, when I was asked to go back to Fulham. One of the directors who I was still familiar with invited me back. John Marshall, one of my old team-mates, was one of the coaches working under Micky

Adams. I made my second debut, as a centre-half in a home game against Darlington, which I think we won handsomely.

Micky wasn't keen on me at all and never hid it. One morning at training I put on a pair of tracksuit bottoms – it was the winter – for the warm-up. He made a big point of sending me back in to get changed. I tried to explain it was just a habit I'd got into at United. Everybody did it. 'That's not what we do here at Fulham,' he said, 'and we're all the same.' I did what he asked, but I don't think I hid the grimace on my face very well. It was strange to return to the place I called home for so long and to be made to feel like I should be completely unfamiliar with it. A lot of the old faces were there and I can't complain about the reaction I got from the fans, then or now. But Micky didn't have time for me, that was obvious, and my heart wasn't in it, so after a few games that too was over. Maybe I should have been better. I should have been more professional and set more of an example, but I knew it was never going to work out with Micky, never in a million years. He called me in for a meeting to formally tell me why he wasn't keeping me on. I wasn't surprised. He called John into the meeting, which I felt was a bit unnecessary and a bit embarrassing, to be told I'm not wanted by the club I grew up in, the club where I grew up alongside John as a kid. I don't think John would have appreciated it.

I got in the car and just drove. I thought, enough is enough. If I couldn't find the feeling at my first club, maybe I was just starting to hate football. Maybe there was a resentment about my injury, that I was owed better. But the saying goes that you only get back what you put in, and I believed in it then just as I do now. I hadn't contributed enough since I left United. My heart hadn't been in anything other than the prospect of that move to Marseille.

After a couple of weeks spent dwelling on things, I was contacted by Gwyn Williams, who had worked in various roles at Chelsea, and I think was either a scout or coach at the time. He said they had a lot of injuries and players on suspensions. They wanted me. *Here's a figure that we'll pay. Just come along and be a part of it.* And I liked that. Honesty – no big promises. It was also something big, exciting and with a direction. The Bosman rule had been implemented so players whose contract had expired had freedom of movement – that rule meant UEFA had to abolish the foreigner rule and, with the Premier League enjoying such a rise to prominence, foreign players were tempted en masse to come to England for the first time. Chelsea had been the club who'd taken advantage of that. They'd signed Roberto Di Matteo, Frank Leboeuf, Gianfranco Zola and Gianluca Vialli – all tempted by the presence of Ruud Gullit, who'd seen out his career as a player at Stamford Bridge and was now the manager. There was a cosmopolitan feel.

All those lads were brilliant, there was a great buzz in the dressing room, and a shared humour. One morning we were showering after training – we were using the Harlington training ground. The showers were always freezing, you needed flip-flops on your feet or you were dying of pneumonia. Chelsea had signed a player called Danny Granville from Cambridge United. Nice lad, very athletic, six-footer, very similar body shape to Lee Sharpe. You could tell he was in a bit of disbelief at the people he was sharing a dressing room with. Danny was in the shower and the next person in was Zola, who started talking to him. Danny was almost in disbelief – *Gianfranco Zola is talking to me.* He was starstruck, and some of the lads, like Dennis Wise, were pissing themselves laughing. Well, unbeknown to Danny, Vialli was standing behind him, literally having a piss against his leg!

The lads were good, but I must admit that my excitement of working with Ruud Gullit quickly fell away. Ruud was one of those players I loved watching. I was a huge fan of the Milan team he'd played in. But the way he spoke to players, particularly the English lads, was with an arrogance I couldn't get on board with. It quickly became apparent to me that, in the emergency, Gwyn had identified me as a player who could do a job, and I was delighted after dropping down the leagues to quickly be back in the Premier League again, but Ruud wouldn't have wanted me there if he'd had any choice in it.

I was professional about it, I was getting myself in decent shape, but Ruud made it obvious that I wasn't really in his plans long-term. I made a few appearances but knew I wouldn't be staying for the long-run. There are just ways about doing things, though, and as Chelsea approached the FA Cup Final they'd qualified for, I had quite an unpleasant experience. I turned up for training at Stamford Bridge on the Friday – we were cutting it fine to travel to the team hotel prior to the final, so I'd made sure I was prepared with my bag and a suit carrier. Ruud named the players who were going and I wasn't included. I looked at Gwyn and he put his fingers to his lips as if to ask me not to say anything. But I said to Gwyn afterwards that I was livid. I'd got guests coming on the tickets I thought I was getting. What was I going to do if I wasn't even at the game? Gwyn couldn't say anything, really. Just that that was the situation.

I'd taken the train in because I presumed I'd be travelling with the team. So I had to go all the way back home, and brooded to myself all day. I decided I'd go anyway, so on the morning of the final I got my partner (now my wife) to drive me to the team hotel. I walked in at breakfast time. A few of the lads were about. There was a big cheer when they saw me. I looked around the room and saw Ruud. I don't know how to describe the look he gave me, but let's just say he was somewhere between annoyed and furious.

It was a completely different feel to going to Wembley with United. With United it's an occasion and everything was done properly. Craig Burley was also out of the squad and he had even more of a reason to be annoyed than I did. He'd scored the goal that got Chelsea to the final and he wasn't even on the bench. He was on the booze right away. He wanted to have it out with Ruud before kick-off and a few of us had to hold him back.

So I'd got myself with the squad but still didn't actually have a ticket to sit in the stands and watch the game. I bumped into Adrian Titcombe, from the FA, and explained the situation. He got tickets for us, so Craig and I were able to sit and watch the match. Craig was getting the worse for wear so we decided to go to a lounge, or what I thought was the players' lounge anyway, only to find that the tickets for the families and guests had been given away by Ken Bates to corporate guests. Nobody was familiar. I went back to Adrian to explain the farce. We went back to sort of see who should and shouldn't be around, and noticed that the few players who were coming in were getting corporate strangers forcing stuff in their face to sign. It just wouldn't have happened at United. It was organised terribly.

Chelsea won the cup. The celebrations went back to the Waldorf Hotel. Again, the players and their wives and partners couldn't even sit down without people coming up with stuff to be signed. We had an incredible venue and it was so badly organised. Then on came the entertainment. Jimmy Tarbuck and Kenny Lynch. I don't think this audience of 19–30s was quite their demographic.

I was in Portugal on holiday recently, having dinner at a golf course. I got a tap on the shoulder. Jimmy Tarbuck. 'Someone mentioned that you were in here.'

'Blimey, Jimmy,' I said, 'you haven't changed … the last time I saw you was 1997 at the Waldorf Hotel.'

'Yeah, I remember,' he says. 'I remember asking my mate, why am I here?!'

Jimmy was good friends with Bobby Campbell, the old Fulham manager whose celebrity pals often ended up at matches. Bobby was pals with Ken. The rest spoke for itself, as nonsensical as it was.

The following morning everyone was getting ready for the open-top bus parade and then to depart for a post-season trip to Thailand. I didn't want to go. Ten days with Ruud Gullit working for a future I didn't want, in a present I didn't want either, didn't appeal very much. I knew my time was up. So I just went straight home from the hotel. And that was it as far as my top-flight career was concerned.

I had a short time playing non-league football, solely because my mates were managing at Heybridge Swifts and Farnborough Town. I played in an Essex Cup game for Heybridge and trained at Farnborough but never even played a minute. That was it. I didn't want to let anybody down, I didn't like drama or a fuss so I didn't deem it necessary to announce my retirement or anything. I'd just lost my drive to play. I was asked to go and train at different places but I knew I'd let myself down and I didn't want to live with that. I couldn't put it all down to Ruud but that experience had soured it for me – I loved him as a player, but to find out how he was as a person soured it for me and made me less enthusiastic about having to go and prove myself in a world where people are expecting certain things based on their own perception. For a little while I'd even almost accepted that I was just going to hate and resent football and blame other people.

You can tell yourself that, but the game is still the game, and because of my clean break and the fact that I'd never really pissed anyone off locally, I still went to non-league matches and was known around the area because of the friendships I'd built. I was invited by Ashford Town to join in the role of director of football, which was a new kind of role that almost seemed to serve an imaginary purpose as far as I was concerned. George

Wakeling was the manager. He was a legend in the local non-league scene, old-school, strong in his decision-making and direction. He didn't need six or seven people around him making decisions and he also had an encyclopaedic knowledge of local players. George had his own assistant so he didn't even really need me helping him on that front.

I'd always been watching non-league football, thanks to my mate Tommy South, who'd owned Purfleet. If I was at Fulham or QPR and had a spare Saturday, even at United if I was down south and had the Saturday, I'd always go to a game. I'd go to their end-of-season events, Ryman League dinners, so I'd had an informal induction into that world and grew to know about the distinct personalities of non-league players and managers. I grew to respect them and the sacrifices they were making for the love of the game. I'd just come out of the professional field but still had so much that was unresolved, so it was good to be surrounded by people who were working hard because they loved it. They weren't professional players. They were blue-collar workers whose livelihood could be impacted by a bad tackle.

Ashford is a big club in a large area of Kent, but everyone was always chasing the land the club was on, and there were financial issues, which sometimes meant you didn't get paid. And people would ask, why do you go if you're not being paid, but you've got your love back for it, and you enjoy being around players again. I just enjoyed training sessions on Tuesday and Thursday nights. They were just lads laughing and joking and I had to remind myself that I had to kind of sit away a little bit because I was meant to be a part of the management. But hearing George talking to a player on the phone and they're apologising because they had to go and see their nan or something, it was just hilarious.

After spending time with George and getting that bit back I started to think, *Do I have something about me that could make me a manager?* I started working as assistant to Gary Bellamy at Chelmsford City. There was no ego and no expectation – anything he wanted from me, I'd do. But Gary got the job at Dover Athletic and the chairman called me to ask me if I'd take the main job at Chelmsford. I admitted I wasn't sure.

'But Paul,' he goes, 'if you say no, then I'll have to bring someone in to do that job and that person is probably going to see Paul Parker as a threat.' He talked a bit more and finished his request off with this statement. 'To be honest Paul, if you don't take the job, I would consider you maybe one of the biggest wankers I've ever known in my life.' He was a well-spoken man with a background in IT. The words didn't suit the mouth they were coming from and made me think differently. I thought, *Right, I'll take it.* And I loved it. After a while, though, the chairman stepped down and another took over – it was obvious from the off that his successor, who'd been vice-chairman, would want his own man. In my last season we won the County Cup, beating two professional sides along the way. In the final, we won 5-0 against the side whose manager would become my successor. At our end-of-season event I decided to jump before I was pushed. I loved the job and I loved my time there but I announced I'd be resigning.

I applied for the manager's position at Welling because it was a family club, and they were good people, but it was a difficult job that came with lofty expectations. The club was close in geography to Charlton and Gillingham, and every time we lost a game I'd get comments about coming from Manchester United. That was par for the course, I suppose, but every day I was having to cross over the Dartford Bridge and drive back through Dartford Tunnel. I was spending more time queueing up there than I was at the training ground. Things became emotionally difficult when my assistant, John Harding, passed away. He'd been a great person to work with. When I eventually appointed a new assistant, it wasn't really the same – he was a player-coach and I had to have conversations about the way we spoke to each other. He didn't take too kindly to it. I brought in Liam Daish, who'd been manager of Havant & Waterlooville. He had a good reputation as far as the style of his teams was concerned and he was a lovely fella. He was honest with his opinions on the team and individuals and he made me better at my job. He'd tell me I needed to speak up more, be bolder.

Really, it probably papered over the cracks, because before long the drain of that travelling started getting to me. I wasn't enjoying it. I was trying to go to watch games and the travelling made it so I was either getting there late or deciding to leave early, or not go at all. I started thinking it would be alright if I missed training because Liam was there. That was an alarm bell for me, because I immediately thought about the better managers I had, and their common theme was that they were always there. I think in my head I'd estimated a non-league boss managing for two nights a week. It was 24/7. I wasn't doing it properly, and when you start to realise that, and you're stretching your time, nobody benefits. The club wasn't getting the best of me. My family weren't either. Every time my boys saw me I was on the phone. We couldn't go out for a meal without my phone constantly going off. I had two phones – my personal phone and my football one. When I went on holiday I left my football phone at home but I still took the sim card. I love football. But that wasn't the life for me.

We lost a midweek game to Eastbourne Borough at home and I wasn't happy, so I said to one of the owners that I had to call it a day. I wasn't feeling it. He asked me to leave it and call him in the morning. I did, but I called him at 7am, as I hadn't been able to sleep. I recommended Liam for the job. They took my advice and he did brilliantly as caretaker. However, they didn't keep him on, which was madness, in my opinion.

I started to watch Gravesend, as the chairman was a big United fan. I recommended Liam for the manager's job there. He did very well. I think he won a couple of trophies there, and it was under his managership that the club went full-time, before they became Ebbsfleet United.

As for me, I'd had my time as a manager. And I'd enjoyed it. It had helped me to rediscover what I loved about the game, and I'd always be grateful for that.

18

Essex, via Singapore, via Darwin

AFTER COMING out of football management I was doing a lot of television punditry work, mostly with Setanta Sports, but when it became clear that the company was having some financial difficulties, I started looking for other opportunities. Someone told me about a new radio station that was opening in New Zealand, dedicated solely to football. I was asked if I wanted to be a part of it. The Premier League was becoming ever more popular, and I always liked the idea of being one of the first to do something, so, after going there and having a look around, I accepted it. My wife was never 100 per cent sold on it, but it promised a good education for the boys and I even accepted a job in a private school where I'd work in PE. Obviously I had no experience, but they promised to help.

We made the trip over in August 2009. I can't remember where the first stop was, but the first in Australia was Darwin. I'd arranged to do an after-dinner in a casino, and we'd stop there for a couple of days on the resort before flying to New Zealand. I did the dinner and then the next day my wife said, bluntly, 'I'm going no further. This is far enough.'

The worst phone call I ever had to make was to call the people in New Zealand to tell them that we wouldn't be going there. I was lucky that I knew some people in the freight business, considering all of our belongings were already in transit. We ended up living in Darwin for eight months. When people think of Australia, they think of Sydney or Brisbane or Melbourne. You think of Darwin, you're thinking of the outback and Ned Kelly. Whenever I mention that I lived in Australia, even to Australians, and I say I lived in Darwin, their first question is always 'why?' In 1974, a cyclone had almost completely destroyed Darwin. There was already a big Greek community that lived locally, but the Greek influence had become particularly notable after the disaster, and a lot of the rebuilt architecture therefore bore those characteristics too.

It was difficult and unfamiliar, particularly for my wife. She could have demanded to go back home, but she didn't. My ego was trying to get through it and I was trying to convince myself that I hadn't made the wrong decision. I tried to get involved with the local football federation but most of my work involved going back and forth to Sydney to work for FOX as a pundit. Eventually we settled in and got to know the locals. Our boys went to school in shorts and T-shirts, and they sang the Australian national anthem every morning. They never complained once.

Regular work with FOX became complicated because of the immigration system in Australia, so it was recommended to me that I apply for residency. So I did, but as part of the process I had to live outside of the shores for two weeks.

Fortunately, I'd also been going over to Singapore to do some punditry work for ESPN, and one of the friends I'd made over there invited me to stay with him while the paperwork was going through.

While I was in Singapore I was contacted by David Rowe, the son of Brian Rowe, who'd been a marketing director at QPR. I met up with Dave and his mates and he suggested to me that I invite my wife and kids over. So they came over for the weekend, and we spent time with Dave and his family. It was all very pleasant, though I missed them when they went back.

A little later, once I was back in Darwin, one of Dave's mates offered me an opportunity to get involved with his business. He said we could move over to Singapore and he'd help with finding a place to live and getting the kids into school. My wife seemed much more happy with Singapore. I defy anyone to not have their breath taken away by the place. It was like a higher form of civilisation. Everything was beautiful. The landscape of the city was like living in the future. Everything was cleaner, more finely tuned, and safer.

I was doing punditry work but got involved with the JSSL (Junior School Soccer League), which had the Arsenal franchise, through Harvey Davis. The Arsenal badge sold it and made it the prominent soccer camp in the locality. I thought initially that I'd just be hanging around but I found myself joining in and getting quite involved even though it was 26 or 27 degrees every day. Constantly sweating. Harvey and I became very good friends. He'd shown great nous and acumen with the school and it continued to grow, eventually becoming the biggest football school in South-East Asia. We ran the biggest youth tournament in the region and named it the Paul Parker trophy. Harvey developed the school and got satellite camps set up – his ambition stretched further, and he asked if I'd contact my old clubs in the UK to help out. I called Mick Phelan – he was back at United coaching, and he and Nicky Butt got involved in bringing a United team out. Arsenal and Spurs followed.

I was happy to help but I was concerned that I was a bit too familiar. I was always there. Everybody knew me now. How could we encourage more people to join? I thought a younger ex-pro might help, and reached out to Andy Cole. Would he mind coming across, being around, hand out the trophies at the end, that sort of thing – he said no problem. He was fantastic. From there, we were able to get Teddy Sheringham, and even Ray Parlour, and it went from strength to strength. It's still going strong today.

My wife made contacts herself and went into business making bespoke perfumes using Oudh from trees around South-East Asia. She worked incredibly hard to make the business a success and now Fragrance Du Bois sells to Harrods and Selfridges, to name just two stores to give an idea of the kind of success she's had.

No matter what, the kids were never a problem. We moved to Darwin and Singapore and they just adapted, got on with other kids and just loved meeting these kids from all over the world.

We missed home, though. We visited and communicated as often as we could, but you always miss out. Then you go home to visit and you can never get round everyone. You call people up to let them know you're home, but people have their own things going on. You get out of sync naturally, and it became very different. But you go back home, your new home in Singapore, and every morning it's at least 24 degrees. You get used to waking up with air conditioning and seeing blue skies almost 90 per cent of the time.

Then the kids went home to the UK – one for college, one for university, and suddenly, everything changes. Their mates go, so their parents did too. They had their own things going on. The bubble you were in disappears. I was going to work more. So was my wife. Then we'd get home and be together and it was the end of another working day. The buzz just drifted away.

My wife's mum fell ill. It got progressively worse, so visits home became more frequent so she could spend more time with her before she passed away. My wife's boss mentioned about her moving back to the UK permanently and, once it was spoken, it made perfect sense. I stayed in Singapore to tie up the outstanding obligations and tried to get back every five or six weeks but it was becoming extremely expensive when my own heart was back with my family. I'd been working and then riding a bike around the island, or working around the clock on anything that would consume my time. It couldn't last. In the summer of 2018 we were all back in the UK for good.

Moving overseas was life-changing for me. It was the second big move of my life, after moving to Manchester. But it was moving overseas that changed my outlook on almost everything, it made me accept my own ignorance and confront the things I took for granted. You make yourself vulnerable in a way where you really become aware of the importance of society. You become aware that it's not about class or social ladders, it's to do with our differences of education, our cultural differences, understanding those and bridging the gap in the most convenient and social ways. I think back to sitting in business meetings with people in Singapore who'd completed university and were running their own companies; I'd be sitting with my JSSL T-shirt and shorts on, having a chat in 28-degree heat, in a bit of shade by the side of a football pitch. You'd get invited to a house that was $12m Singapore dollars and the people you're speaking to are just ordinary people without any air of superiority.

I think once you venture out into a land where you have communication barriers and you're relying on the most simple forms of communication to get by, you become extremely aware and conscious about the detail of your own behaviour, the consequences of your words and actions, the responsibility you have. It's a mirror to yourself and makes you more willing to accept how wrong you can be. You could say all of our experiences change us. I was changed from when I was a youngster in London and I moved to Manchester and then I changed again afterwards. There are the other bits that are important, the fact that going to the biggest club in the world opens doors to things you just wouldn't even comprehend. Sometimes my wife and I consider the alternative, if we hadn't moved abroad, but I think of her career now and the amazing things she's achieved, I think of the friendships the boys have made with people around the world, and I certainly wouldn't change it.

One thing that being displaced does is give you a different perspective of time, and the value of it. Death brings that home. I never lived in the pocket of my parents. From the age of 15, they were used to me being away and popping in, saying hello and getting out. After everything they did to provide a good life for me and my siblings, my parents still live in the same house they were in that George Best dropped me off at. They bought it from the council as a two-bedroom and now it's a four-bedroom house with a garage on the side. They've been in that house since I was five. I've never spent a night in there since I left home. I couldn't even tell you why. I can go around to drop my grandkids off to see them but I just can't hang around.

When I was abroad, the biggest difficulty for me was not seeing my daughter as often as I'd have liked. I try to make up for it now. She's very much like me – very strong-minded, very opinionated. I've learned when to talk and when not to, because I know I won't win. She gave me two fantastic grandchildren and she loves my parents. I think she knows more about my own mum than I do.

Your ego changes when you get older. When I went to Manchester, I think some changes in my personality were not for the better. My mates would comment on me being cocky. They didn't push it too far – I don't think they wanted to genuinely offend me, they just wanted to point it out. In the moment, well, I can't say it's offence, but it's something you take to heart. You don't want to have changed, because that's meant to be a negative thing. But you get older and you realise that all these experiences are designed to change you. How can you go to Manchester United and not be changed? How can you go to Manchester United and not *want* to be changed? Wouldn't 99 out of 100 people say that? Still, it gets brought up occasionally even now. And you can't help but cringe. But you do change. And a lot of change is growth.

I live back down south now. It would have been easy for me to go back to Manchester once I was back in the UK but there's a part of me that likes that it's a bit far away. Okay, the city has changed. It's probably a bit too much like London now for my liking, but not enough that this buzz I get whenever I arrive in the city is affected. Yeah, a little bit of ego massaging helps now and again. But I love Manchester as a place.

We could put that down to nostalgia, and a time of my life that I loved. I wasn't the only one. There were so many of us who were really lucky to be chosen by the manager to be a part of that historic moment. Our chapter in history was unique – part of the first dominant Manchester United team after the Busby era, a team that won medals at a rate that compared with the greatest in the club's history. The privilege to be part of that lineage is something beyond my comprehension.

As I consider how to summarise that and close off this book, I have to be honest. There's still a wrinkle, you know. It bothers me a little that I never won more. Is that greed talking? I mean, I'm satisfied. I'm pleased with and proud of that record. But in a strange way I'm prouder still to have that bit about me, that residual hunger. That's a part of my character that I know was instilled in me by the boss. He burrowed into my instinct and intertwined a winning mentality with my perception of survival. If you didn't have that, you weren't lasting at the club. I carry that with me as proudly as I do any of my winner's medals.